JOHN F. KENNEDY AND NEW FRONTIER DIPLOMACY, 1961–1963

JOHN F. KENNEDY AND NEW FRONTIER DIPLOMACY, 1961–1963

Timothy P. Maga

KRIEGER PUBLISHING COMPANY
MALABAR, FLORIDA
1994

Original Edition 1994

Printed and Published by
KRIEGER PUBLISHING COMPANY
KRIEGER DRIVE
MALABAR, FLORIDA 32950

FROM A DECLARATION OF PRINCIPLES JOINTLY ADOPTED BY A COMMITTEE
OF THE AMERICAN BAR ASSOCIATION AND A COMMITTEE OF PUBLISHERS:

This publication is designed to provide accurate and authoritative information in regard
to the subject matter covered. It is sold with the understanding that the publisher is
not engaged in rendering legal, accounting, or other professional service. If legal advice
or other expert assistance is required, the services of a competent professional person
should be sought.

Library of Congress Cataloging-In-Publication Data

Maga, Timothy P., 1952–
   John F. Kennedy and New Frontier diplomacy, 1961–1963 / by Timothy
P. Maga.
     p. cm.
   Includes bibliographical references (p.) and index.
   ISBN 0-89464-829-2 (acid-free paper)
   1. United States—Foreign relations—1961–1963. 2. Kennedy, John
F. (John Fitzgerald), 1917–1963. I. Title.
E841.M23 1993
327.73′009′046—dc20   92-43248
                                                    CIP

10 9 8 7 6 5 4 3 2

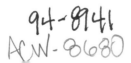

CONTENTS

PREFACE

Flaunting his youth with self-assured charm, he called us to do great things and we listened. Some even acted, for his was to be a special presidency. With a band of hard-nosed yet passionate loyalists at his side, John Fitzgerald Kennedy elevated idealism to a pinnacle position in government policy making. Nowhere was this idealism more apparent than in American foreign affairs. War, tyranny, disease, and poverty itself were the common enemies of mankind, the young president said. Through the "noble calling" of politics, he asked even younger Americans to join him in battling these enemies. The Peace Corps became his most lasting bequest within this call to action, but there were other policies and an especial abundance of ideas.

More than one hundred years before Kennedy's New Frontier, the intensely idealistic and Massachusetts-based transcendentalist movement observed that "the past was a foreign country. People do things differently there." Thirty years after Kennedy's Camelot, both hindsight and history suggested that New Frontier idealism was a mistake. Kennedy's "pay any price, bear any burden" inaugural pledge was based on his recent memory of World War II victories and the legacy of American invincibility. This cocky self-confidence, it has been said, bred diplomatic arrogance and the disaster of Vietnam. Single-minded careerism and public apathy grew out of that disaster, while activist government took the full blame. Thus, the Peace Corps became synonymous with unrealistic, even foolish foreign policy, and new Peace Corps volunteers went overseas to help isolated, individual communities and not their country.

Indeed, the adoring crowd at the 1961 inaugural would have been shocked to hear a mid-1980s commencement speech at Harvard University, Kennedy's alma mater, whereby greed was praised as "good" and the graduates cheered. Kennedy's New Frontier had given way to the Me Decade and the Gimme Decade, where discussions on the shrinking limits of American power remained more common than talk of international commitments, influence, and volunteerism. My book examines Kennedy's self-proclaimed "great adventure," i.e., his foreign policy. It always represented the loftiest goals of his administration. Yet, be it Latin American or Pacific policy, free trade, or Vietnam, Kennedy and his "best and brightest" team often failed to translate their vision into practical policy. It would be their failures, inherited by succeeding administrations, that would help lead America away from the era of public action to the era of self-absorption.

The tale of Camelot has been told many times, from Arthur Schlesinger's postassassination period analysis of the inner workings of the Kennedy White House to *The National Enquirer's* 1980s denunciations of the late president's sexual mores. Kennedy's foreign policy has been a text topic for former Kennedy staffers, and it has appeared in edited works of historical essays. This book, as a historical narrative, will try to pull together the many visionary plans, crisis management traumas, practical policy struggles, and inherent contradictions of the Kennedy foreign policy. It is in no way the final word on the matter.

The Kennedy presidency no longer appears synonymous with foreign policy change and innovation. Most of the changes came after the New Frontier was over. Indeed, following Kennedy's assassination, "the torch" was not even "passed to a new generation of Americans," for his immediate Oval Office successors were all older than he. Yet, in January 1961, America awaited a revolution of sorts. Kennedy promised "to get America moving again," and this included destroying America's "Ugly American" image abroad, winning the allegiance of the Third World, and total victory in the cold war by 1970. Vigor and brains would become the real weapons of diplomacy, replacing the "worn out" policies of the Eisenhower administration. At last, Arthur Schlesinger, Jr., a historian and Kennedy staffer remembered, "intelligence was being applied to public affairs. Euphoria reigned; we thought for a moment that the world was plastic and the future unlimited." It survived for a thousand days.

In the 1990s, few associate "intelligence" with Kennedy's decisions to escalate America's military presence in Vietnam, to accelerate the nuclear arms race, to play brinkmanship over Cuba, and to attempt to maneuver a variety of nations to fit his cold war objectives. On the other hand, Kennedy established a Nuclear Test Ban Treaty as a first step toward nuclear disarmament, contemplated military withdrawal from Vietnam, as well as worried if his own cold war rhetoric had not brought the world closer to World War III and to an eternal "Ugly American" image abroad. Both the man and his foreign policy decisions were complex and sometimes bizarre. Nevertheless, his vision for a better America and world still raises positive images in an era of declining superpower strength and rising Japan. It is because of this new reality that Kennedy's era of vigor, commitment, and unassailable American military/economic power has become very alien to some and nostalgic to others. Today, both Democrats and Republicans hope that a candidate with locks of hair falling in his eyes, a tightly buttoned suit, a forever pointing finger, and an acceptably eloquent stammer will remind the voters of Kennedy and greatness. Yet, Kennedy was always more intricate than these images, and greatness need not be relegated to the 1960s.

Currently, much of America's view of Kennedy, and especially Kennedy the foreign policy maker, is provided by the prolific Thomas Paterson, a University of Connecticut–Storrs professor of history. Paterson, in one of his best books of edited essays, *Kennedy's Quest for Victory* (New York: Oxford University Press, 1989), presents Kennedy as a dangerous and reckless cold war extremist more concerned about his career than the nation and world responsibilities. This argument is partially accepted by another academic, David Burner, in his brief, general account entitled *John F. Kennedy and a New Generation* (Glenview, IL: Scott, Foresman and Co., 1988). According to Burner, Kennedy was dangerous and reckless, but also a confused liberal with a sex hangup. Both Paterson and Burner accept the thesis of an earlier analysis as fact, namely Henry Fairlie's *The Kennedy Promise: The Politics of Expectation* (Garden City, NY: Doubleday, 1973). Fairlie argued that Kennedy's positive image in the public memory was unjustified and unnecessary, for he had accomplished too little as president.

These studies contrast greatly to the glowing memoirs of Kennedy staffers, such as Schlesinger, Theodore Sorensen, Pierre Salinger, and others. Enthralled by the promise of the New Frontier and American invincibility, they saw the Kennedy era as their finest hour. Later analysts would find something hideous in their attraction to Kennedy, and their observations were soon rejected as partisan and foolish. My book has no intention of adoring a murdered president or castigating him as an especially dangerous aberration in American foreign policy-making. There is at place for vision, ideas, and well-intentioned debate in American history. Kennedy enjoyed the politics of vision, and Americans more than a generation later remember this "Kennedy promise" with fondness. For that alone, Kennedy's foreign policy merits a closer look. In an era of soul-searching over America's collapsing influence in world affairs, a fresh analysis of New Frontier diplomacy can only assist those who believe in "getting America moving again" and who want to avoid the errors of the 1960s.

CHAPTER 1

Searching for the New Frontier

"People will remember not only what he did but what he stood for," Theodore Sorensen noted a generation after John Kennedy's successful run for the presidency. "He had confidence in man and gave men confidence in the future. Just as no chart on the history of weapons could accurately reflect the advent of the atom, so it is my belief that no scale of good and bad Presidents can rate John Fitzgerald Kennedy."[1] Beleaguered by attacks on his former boss's cold war extremism, sexual mores, and policy-making pragmatism, Sorensen, who served as Kennedy's special counsel, struck back at the critics. They have not gone away, and neither have those who claim that Kennedy "still stirs the passions of those who find little inspiration in other symbols, other men, other Presidents."[2]

Both the critics and the myth-makers rarely separate Kennedy's domestic policies from his foreign affairs endeavors. The purveyors of praise and condemnation usually build their arguments within a general thesis, prompting old New Frontiersmen, like Sorensen, to elevate their late hero above them all. In reality, there is little reason to elevate the Kennedy White House's foreign policy machinery above that of its predecessors or its successors. Kennedy and his youthful diplomatic colleagues were attracted to experimental government. They admitted that they hoped to "find themselves" through innovative foreign policies. In their best personal image, Kennedy and his foreign policy team saw themselves as an antibureaucratic bureaucracy, a working think tank that did not want to be called a think tank. A government of programmed good intentions, programmed doubt, and unpredictability, the Kennedy administration pushed American foreign policy making to the threshold of chaos, but never quite jumped over the edge.

The 1960s perception of Kennedy's greatness as a foreign policy crisis manager versus the ever-growing 1970s-to-the-present perception of Kennedy, the foreign policy-making enigma, harkens back to 1960 campaign expectations. To the historians and Kennedy advisors, James MacGregor Burns and Arthur Schlesinger, Jr., Kennedy's 1960 promise was present in the hope that the young candidate would be a transcending leader, a moral leader, a new FDR who would redesign both the Democratic party and America's place in the world. These expectations were incredibly high. Both Burns and Schlesinger were aware, given their published analyses of previous presidents and their own investigations of Kennedy, that the 1960 Democratic presidential candidate was a centrist, a pragmatist, and an ambitious Massachusetts senator.[3] Yet, this was only one side of the Kennedy reality, they said, and many shared this view.

State after state, and nearly minute to minute, Kennedy's 1960 campaign spoke of "moving America forward again" and rescuing the nation from the weary, fearful old men of the Dwight Eisenhower administration. Consequently, Kennedy set his own high expectations. More than twenty years earlier, as a Harvard history major, Kennedy had studied presidential politics under Dr. Arthur Holcombe, the renowned humanitarian. Thanks to Holcombe, Kennedy maintained a healthy respect for cautious presidential leadership. Still, Kennedy was also impressed by the work of Dr. Richard Neustadt who praised presidential activism and the accomplishments of FDR's frenetic New Deal diplomacy. In the early 1960s, Kennedy's fellow Harvard graduates, Burns and Schlesinger, saw the possibility of Kennedy marrying the pragmatic concerns of Holcombe and the activist stress of Neustadt into one presidential administration. Foreign policy would be the best vehicle to demonstrate the great powers of the presidency.[4] But did Kennedy entertain such a marriage?

IDEOLOGY AND FOREIGN POLICY

Throughout his presidency, Kennedy would wrestle with the ideological aspects of foreign policy and how, if ever, they should be practically applied. Indeed, as early as the 1960 campaign, there were two forces tugging at Kennedy. On the one hand, he hoped to be the classic Jefferson-Wilson model of a president. That meant staying loyal to the general concerns of his party, handling foreign policy crises as they came up with a certain expediency, and providing strong, well-announced moral leadership for America in the world arena. This bespoke a commitment to the presidency's best traditions, he believed, even though Jefferson regarded himself a poor president who had led America closer to "Mr. Madison's War" of 1812, and even though Wilson defeated his best visionary policy, the Versailles Treaty, through an inability to deal with Congress. During the 1960 campaign, Kennedy, with a splash of patriotic eloquence, consistently praised Jefferson and Wilson as great presidential role models. His comments were formulated to suggest, beyond the election rhetoric, that the 1960s equaled the era of the all-powerful, unassailable president. Nevertheless, that very suggestion disturbed him, and the second classic model, that of the quiet, bipartisan president, tugged at him as well.[5]

In late 1960, Kennedy told MacGregor Burns that a truly activist president might lead America to World War III and nuclear destruction. Did a president have to be so strongly committed to cold war rhetoric that nuclear war was inevitable? Presidential leadership, he noted, had limits, but that did not mean he would stop "imparting" presidential energy and Free World stewardship. If he could pull together his own cabinet and Congress, and strengthen the dialogue with America's anticommunist allies, a "team" would be truly established to continue the challenge against communism. That would be good enough, he concluded, and politically acceptable to America "for two presidential terms."[6]

The interest in working with a dedicated group of "team" players stemmed from Kennedy's days as a spindly, but determined member of the Harvard football team. Drilled by his hard-nosed, yet loving father, Ambassador Joseph Kennedy, he was expected "never to shrink in the face of adversity." The future president once continued to play football after fracturing his leg. On another occasion, he ruptured a spinal disc, but also continued to play. Later questioned about the logic of these decisions, Kennedy simply replied, "We won."

Kennedy's early commitment to competition even included his romantic interludes, whereby in the late 1930s, while serving as a naval intelligence officer in Washington, D.C., he competed for the attentions of Inga Arvad. Considered one of Europe's most beautiful women, Arvad, a former Miss Denmark and a once-rumored mistress of Adolf Hitler, supported a variety of pro-Nazi causes in America. The Kennedy-Arvad liaison prompted an FBI investigation of the former's daily activities. Kennedy was labeled a possible pro-Nazi security risk, and the FBI helped engineer his transfer to seamanship school in northern Illinois and then PT-boat service in the Pacific. He never believed that an apology was in order for the Arvad affair, especially since he defeated Arvad's suitors and won her charms. All, as the saying goes, remained fair in love and war. Yet, Kennedy's PT-boat experience during World War II changed him. His interest in competitiveness and the swiftest path to victory continued, but his associates were no longer always the comfortable rich.[7] In August 1943, following the ramming of his PT-109 by a Japanese destroyer in Blackett Strait west of New Georgia, Kennedy owed his life to a cross-section of American middle- and working-class Navy personnel as well as to poor Pacific islanders. He never forgot that fact or the new "team" that he had discovered. Through war, he had learned how the other half lives and dies. On September 12, 1943, he wrote to his parents that his months in the Pacific would have a lasting impact on his life.

> When I read that we will fight the Japs for years if necessary and will sacrifice hundreds of thousands if we must—I always like to check from where he is talking—it's seldom out here [Pacific islands]. People get too used to talking about billions of dollars and millions of soldiers that thousands of dead sound like a drop in the bucket. But if those thousands want to live as much as the ten [PT-109 crewmen] I saw—they should measure their words with great, great care.[8]

Although he had discovered the common man in the 1940s, and thought that he might be part of their team now, that team had no immediate impact on the Kennedy outlook for a better world and America's place in it. As a congressman from Cambridge, Massachusetts, in the late 1940s, he depicted himself as a "fighting conservative," even though war injury and Addison's disease had made him look too gaunt to fight a soul. Indeed, it was that very gauntness, coupled with youthful jabs against the Democratic party of his father's generation, that helped him win election. Most ignored his talk of "new ideas" in policy making, for he never defined the ideas or the policies. Yet, the "new ideas" slogan was attractive, and it distracted voters from the fact that he was still the very wealthy son of the very wealthy Joseph Kennedy.[9] Meanwhile, he jousted against the aging leadership of the Cambridge veteran's associations to the delight of the crowd.

None of Kennedy's 1946 campaign rhetoric translated into innovative suggestions, or legislation sponsored, on behalf of a "new ideas" foreign policy. During the late 1940s, Representative Kennedy reflected the cold war concerns of the conservatives in both major political parties. Communism, he said, was a global threat and was reaching America's shores. Franklin Roosevelt had "sold out" Eastern Europe during the 1945 Yalta conference with Churchill and Stalin, President Harry Truman had "lost China," and Senator Joseph McCarthy's (R-Wis.) Senate Un-American Affairs Committee was trying to rescue America's State and Defense Departments from internal subversion.[10]

Nevertheless, Kennedy confused his electorate and general observers, often implying through his actions that the only members of his particular team were himself. For Kennedy's sake, this was a cruel judgment, for the most significant political posture for him in the late 1940s and early 1950s involved breaking away from his father's old-fashioned conservatism. For instance, John Kennedy supported the Truman Doctrine's commitment to halt expanding communism around the world through economic, political, and military interventions. Joseph Kennedy, who had opposed the interventionist attractions of FDR's New Deal and had supported Britain's search for appeasement to Hitler before World War II, saw Truman as an upstart Wilsonian. "This C student in High School" [Truman], Joe Kennedy believed, was more concerned about challenging communism than assessing its cost. John Kennedy found the challenge more important, and also welcomed the expensive Marshall Plan for postwar European economic recovery.[11]

Joe Kennedy thought communism was too divisive and too struggling to be considered a monolithic threat to America, and, therefore, the country could afford to do nothing. Jack Kennedy saw dishonor in doing nothing, and questioned all those who thought that a concerted, united democratic front of allies against communism would more strongly unite the communists and invite World War III. They were strong already, he argued, and they would not wither in the face of American inaction. Hence, the son was breaking away from his father's definition of conservative foreign policy, whereby the old Hoover-Stimson Doctrine of nonrecognition to despicable foreign policies made by despicable men was more important than attacking them. The Boston press was taken aback. Jack Kennedy was not necessarily his father's son; however, he was not a postwar mover and shaker in foreign policy matters either.[12]

As he contemplated running for a Senate seat during the dark days of the Korean War and Senator McCarthy's "Red baiting" zenith, John Kennedy returned to his late 1930s-style womanizing. He could be seen on Capitol Hill for no more than two to two-and-one-half days per week, and rumors suggested that he preferred bed to bantering with his congressional colleagues and staff. The Senate race promised to be a rough one, for his opponent was an incumbent institution in Massachusetts politics, Senator Henry Cabot Lodge, Jr. With a mixture of majority party visibility and a grass roots campaign that contacted each voter twice, Kennedy always had enjoyed a chance of victory in 1952. It was his stress on foreign policy issues that gave him the edge. Kennedy accused Lodge of being too soft on communism by emphasizing Lodge's faith in the United Nations and international, FDR-styled conference diplomacy. An international crisis, Lodge believed, could be averted or resolved by stronger American input via international diplomacy. Kennedy denounced Lodge as a foolish visionary who sacrificed the everyday concerns of Massachusetts residents to internationalist dreams.[13]

Yet Kennedy's attacks on Lodge were not couched in the classic McCarthyite Red scare approach. Instead, he offered a polished, eloquent appeal in favor of American national self-interest abroad and giving the Truman Doctrine more chances to succeed. It was a welcome relief from the pedestrian anticommunist shouting matches of a Senator McCarthy, but many Democrats outside of Massachusetts wondered if the Kennedy approach was simply a new East Coast version of Wisconsin-based McCarthyism. Governor Adlai Stevenson of Illinois, the unsuccessful 1952 and 1956 Democratic presidential candidate, even complained that Kennedy's eloquent McCarthyism was "pap for swooning housewives."[14]

In any event, Kennedy remained a winning candidate and Stevenson a loser, making it easy for the confident Massachusetts politician to discuss the latter's comments. Kennedy squeaked by Lodge with a seventy thousand vote margin, after seeing to it that nearly all of Massachusetts' voters had received a fat brochure detailing his World War II exploits. Lodge's alleged aloofness to cold war confrontation with the Soviet Union was especially accented in the brochure. After the Lodge defeat, Kennedy, already thinking of a 1960s presidency, praised his opponent for defending international diplomacy. In an effort to move more toward a political center, he toned down his anticommunist remarks. During the Senate vote of censure in 1954 against Joe McCarthy and his unethical tactics against accused procommunist American bureaucrats, Kennedy condemned several of McCarthy's aides as extremists. Given his father's still strong admiration for McCarthy, his brother Robert's former staff position with the McCarthy office, and the concern among some conservatives that McCarthy was hounded by less-than-patriotic liberal critics, Kennedy tried to avoid straightforward constituent questions on whether he was pro- or anti-McCarthy. Meanwhile, he abandoned his "most eligible bachelor" status in Washington and married the elegant daughter of millionaire financier John Bouvier, Jacqueline. He now considered himself, conveniently, a married gentleman. A married gentleman did not attack fellow senators when they were down.[15]

The marriage, rather divorced from romantic concerns, assured Kennedy a new prominence in the *Social Register*, for it took away the rich, skirt-chasing bad boy image that sometimes haunted him in Massachusetts politics and, perhaps, even accounted for vote loss. He was "royalty now," he joked with his brothers Robert and Edward, and he compared himself to the central characters of John Buchan's *Pilgrim's Way*. That work praised the combination of wealthy elitism and philanthropic interests which guided the upper-class political community of colonial England. Bachelor politicians did not succeed in Buchan's book. With the proper wife at his side, Kennedy could project the more acceptable public image of the wealthy, concerned young intellectual-cum-politician.[16] Jacqueline, outside of wealth and beauty, could claim an educational pedigree that included Miss Porter's School, Vassar, and the Sorbonne. Mrs. Kennedy could even be of use in formulating foreign policy. It was Jacqueline who provided her husband with English translations of French highbrow analyses of the French Vietnam and Algerian crises in the early to mid 1950s. Indeed, her work, which always offered the harshest translations possible against the excesses of French power, helped sway Senator Kennedy to oppose the idea of sending United States forces to Vietnam in 1954.[17]

The French effort to defeat communism in Vietnam, he told the press, was a smokescreen to cover nineteenth century-style French colonial policies there.[18] Few paid any attention to his comments at the time, but they were part of an effort to distance himself from his waning

McCarthyite image and embrace a politically acceptable "new directions" theme. The fact that his position against United States military
intervention came too late to matter, near the time of the French defeat
at Dien Bien Phu, made that theme acceptable.

Mrs. Kennedy's efforts to educate her husband on the issue of French
colonial pomposity remained unrecognized. Her role as translator-pro-
vider at home, and symbol of female elegance abroad, equaled the limits
of female emancipation for Senator Kennedy.[19] He had no interest in
delegating policy-making powers to his spouse, as FDR had done for
Eleanor Roosevelt on several occasions. Kennedy's own personal outlook on women, largely inherited from a playboy father and influenced
by the culture of the times, was that women, especially wives, made
lousy diplomats. Privately, he criticized Eleanor Roosevelt's "harping"
at the United Nations on humanitarian issues, and he particularly opposed her effort to create a more generous "open door" policy in re-
gards to refugee entry into the United States. The latter would disturb
the progress of organized labor, he complained. Returning the fire, the
former First Lady criticized Kennedy's "lack of courage" to assault and
weed out the lingering vestiges of McCarthyism in public policy. A
better world, she believed, remained distant as long as militant cold war
rhetoric dominated American foreign policy-making decisions.[20]

Throughout his public life, Kennedy claimed to admire the brave new
projects of brave women. He had kind words for Eleanor Roosevelt in
several speeches, and he often praised the analytical powers of historian
Barbara Tuchman and her analysis of the collapsing diplomacy of the
Great Powers during the era of the First World War. Yet, he would
never have these women, or those like them, within his policy-making
"team." Given a different set of circumstances, he believed he could
duplicate their work and do it better. A healthy sense of intellectual
inquiry, always relevant to Kennedy, permitted him to accept their work
and argue their merits. He did not have to accept or employ the architects of these works.[21]

PROFILES IN COURAGE
MEETS THE UGLY AMERICAN

Eleanor Roosevelt's attack on Kennedy's "lack of courage" was a
living irony to the man who won the 1957 Pulitzer Prize for his book,

Profiles in Courage. Kennedy's book of historical essays, first published in 1956, was the product of his own haphazard rough drafts, but the work was organized and honed by his publicist Ted Sorensen. Rumors still abound whether the Kennedy family paid off the Pulitzer Committee in the interest of making John more marketable as a brilliant presidential hopeful. Others suggest that the Committee gave the Pulitzer to Kennedy in an orgy of pro-Democratic party sentiment, even though they knew that Sorensen did most of the work.[22] Most likely, they just liked the book. Campaign-related texts, and the question of who writes them, would become an especially strong ethical dilemma for a later generation more concerned about moral/political connections. As late as 1984, when Senator Gary Hart (D-Col.) established a special staff section in his Capitol Hill office to write a book on the Hart view of United States-Asian-Pacific policy, few really cared that Hart had no hand in its writing or that it carried only one author's name, Hart. Most were concerned with its content.[23]

Profiles in Courage did not dissect the mechanics of American foreign policy, but it offered basic themes for the coming Kennedy agenda. It also reflected more of Sorensen's liberal bias than Kennedy's vision. Dedicated to the memory of another Massachusetts politician, John Quincy Adams, the text suggested that the dreams and aspirations of the disastrous Adams administration of 1825–1829 were more important than its accomplishments. Envisioning an expansionist foreign policy with a sense of democratic mission beyond the Monroe Doctrine which he wrote, Adams led a Third World-like nation obsessed with the desire for practical government and westward settlement. More at home discussing the fortunes of European politics than examining the economic struggles of common Americans, Adams still believed that American slavery and racism might disappear in time through new education programs. Be it a stronger position for America in the world arena or heading off domestic civil war through gentlemanlike dialogue and long-term projects, Adams favored taking "the first step" toward a stronger nation.

To Sorensen and Kennedy, promising the electorate an Adams-styled "first step" to unassailable American greatness and victory in the cold war equaled the best political tactic for the coming new decade. Although there was much truth to their portrait of Adams, it was an image that they largely built for themselves.[24]

The first application of Kennedy's "first step" politics came in October 1957 in his official reaction to the Soviet launching of the Sputnik satellite. Whereas others, including future presidential rival, Senator Hubert Humphrey (D-Minn.), attacked Soviet secrecy and treachery, Kennedy won national attention over his assault on the American public school system. He blamed it for failing to provide scientists and thinkers who could have already created an American space program. New commitments to education, as an Adams might have said, constituted "the first step" to a stronger anticommunist challenge as well as to a successful space program.[25]

Despite a record of supporting legislative measures that took steps backward, such as legalized racism in the southern United States Kennedy, again like the Adams of *Profiles in Courage*, said that he still had faith in the American school system's capability to rail against the evils of racism. That capability could be enhanced through greater government support. Hence, he continued to predict that in less than a generation's time both domestic racism and international communism would be conquered.[26] The prediction offered him a mildly liberal image, thanks to favorable press analysis. This effort to defuse the young senator's McCarthyite reputation also remained the brainchild of Sorensen, and it brought him closer to the truly acceptable mainstream of the Democratic party.

Appealing to that mainstream and winning them to his "team" would remain a difficult task for the retired "fighting conservative," unless he found the "right key." By the late 1950s, Kennedy rhetoric maintained a consistent theme. Even as an undeclared presidential candidate, he promised to "lift us beyond our capacities" and "give the country back to its best self, wiping away the world's impression of an old nation of old men, weary, played out, fearful of the future. . . . " Thus, he hoped "to teach mankind that the process of rediscovering America is not over."[27] From the perspective of a generation later, this rhetoric smacks of a certain unfashionable political arrogance. From the Kennedy perspective of the late 1950s, it was the best "right key" theme to employ. It hit a responsive chord.

The term "right key" came from the 1958 best seller (five million copies), *The Ugly American*, by Captain William Lederer, U.S.N., and Dr. Eugene Burdick, a political science professor, Kennedy was one of its early readers. He made its thesis his own, and it fit well with his *Profiles in Courage* image making. Dissecting American foreign policy, and particularly United States–Southeast Asian relations, in the form of a political thriller, *The Ugly American* was originally attacked by literary and political critics as "hurried," "comic book simplicity," and "epic nonsense."[28] This was not the conclusion of reading America. Although their text remained a series of foreign policy vignettes, Burdick and Lederer consistently bemoaned the "passing of American power" in the world, and especially in the Asian Third World. It was there, they said, in the shadow of Mao Tse-Tung's new China, where the cold war would be won or lost.[29]

Catching up with their constituents, Capitol Hill's foreign policy-making machinery began to credit Lederer and Burdick with "great insights" by 1959. Senator William Fulbright (D-Ark.) of the Senate Foreign Relations Committee attacked the Eisenhower administration's record of foreign aid to "tinhorn dictators" in Asia. He began an investigation to ascertain whether military aid, as opposed to economic aid, was actually harming American anticommunist interests in Asia. Meanwhile, Senator Stuart Symington (D-Missouri), pondering a run for the presidency himself, introduced a bill to create a foreign service academy modeled after West Point. An antiintellectual, McCarthyite extremism guided the foreign service bureaucracy, he noted. "Transfusing Main Street into the U.S. Foreign Service" through this bill, he concluded, would reform American foreign policy making and end the endless "diplomatic stumbles" abroad. Eventually considered a boondoggle and a plan for a redundant foreign service training school, the so-called "Ugly American Bill" was defeated by Symington's colleagues.[30]

Kennedy, as always, kept his cool on public controversies, and the "Ugly American" matter was no different. He watched his potential 1960 opponents bury themselves in overreaction. Lederer and Burdick had had no easy cures for "diplomatic stumbles," and Kennedy understood that admission well. To Lederer and Burdick, American diplomats were uniformly more stupid than Soviet ones. Noting that America, since 1945, had long demonstrated its "greatness" in the Third World through military power, the two authors wondered whatever happened to American "goodness." "Poor America," one of their fictional characters observed. "It took the British a hundred years to lose their prestige in Asia. America has managed to lose hers in ten years. . . . She could get it all back in two years."[31]

The loss of prestige, Lederer and Burdick pointed out, was directly linked to John Foster Dulles's "bigger bang for the buck" nuclear diplomacy as well as to his view of a monolithic communist conspiracy.

Dulles was secretary of state to President Eisenhower for nearly two terms. His solution to outside or internal communist pressures or a noncommunist Third World regime involved threatening nuclear retaliation against the major instigators of those pressures, namely China and the Soviet Union. Moreover, Third World efforts to play both sides of the cold war in the interest of winning the highest foreign economic aid package was considered procommunist "treachery" by Dulles. Championed by Third World government leaders from Egypt's Nassar to Indonesia's Sukarno, this "treacherous" doctrine of nonalignment encouraged Third World neutrality in the cold war. Dulles saw commitment to American-defined anticommunism as the only possible policy for Third World nations. There could be no neutrality. Although Eisenhower had his doubts about this approach, he supported his secretary of state. It appeared to be consistent with the original hard-line Truman doctrine precedent, and, therefore, remained written in stone.[32] If handled properly, it could become an easy target for Kennedy to attack. *The Ugly American* provided a springboard for that attack.

Nothing should be sacred in foreign policy making, Lederer and Burdick warned their readers. Innovation was more important than guidelines, they suggested; however, policy innovations were not volunteered in their text. *The Ugly American* could be interpreted as an appeal to tone down the anticommunist mission and pay closer attention to the economic needs of poor Third World residents. That attention might require Washington to reassess the military priorities of the Third World. American indifference to Third World commoners, and to the proper administration of aid programs for them, strengthened rather than lessened the appeal of communism. These types of conclusions, some believed, equaled the bottom line of *The Ugly American* thesis. Kennedy did not see it that way, and his view was closer to the authors' intentions.[33] The *Ugly American* was concerned about finding the proper tactic to win the Third World to the American anticommunist cause. Caring for the downtrodden was not the object of their call for new, innovative policies. Those policies would always be attached to national self-interest priorities. Halting the spread of communism remained the primary objective. Hence, the best, most innovative American foreign policy-maker in the Third World would be one who "knew how to go off into the countryside and show the idea of America to the people. . . . Every person and every nation has a key to open their hearts. If you use the right key, you can maneuver any person, or any nation any way you want."[34]

A little more than two years after the appearance of Lederer and Burdick's book, Kennedy would be asking Americans "to ask what they can do for their country." The answers, he soon demonstrated, were in the Peace Corps and the Special Forces, or in the more bureaucratic Alliance for Progress and New Pacific Community projects to maneuver Third World opinion. Yet before he reached Camelot, Kennedy won further attention in the late 1950s for his many "Letters to the Editor," praising *The Ugly American* in the major newspapers and journals of the nation. Criticized at the time, and especially later, for not fully examining Lederer and Burdick's work, Kennedy ignored the critics. Indeed, Kennedy had little interest in dissecting theses. His major concern was wedding his own foreign policy rhetoric to an unusually popular book, and doing it better than any of his potential rivals for the presidency. From the hindsight of twenty years, Arthur Schlesinger admitted that *The Ugly American* provided the Kennedy team with both a campaign salvo to level against the Republicans as well as plenty of illusions over the making of U.S. foreign policy. We "had a romantic view of the possibilities of diplomacy," he remembered.

> We wanted to replace protocol-minded, striped-pants officials by reform-minded missionaries of democracy who mixed with the people, spoke the native dialects, ate the food, and involved themselves in local struggles against ignorance and want. This view had its most genial expression in the Peace Corps, its most corrupt in the mystique of counter-insurgency.[35]

Kennedy judged *The Ugly American*'s popularity quite adequately. The public's perception that American foreign policy needed a facelift became Kennedy's perception as well. As long as he promised "first steps" to remedying Third World problems, he never had to outline precisely where he stood on the facelift issue. Sorensen polished his rhetoric on the matter, and he won new assistance from Representative Henry Reuss. A young Democratic congressman from Milwaukee with a Ph.D. in economics, Reuss counseled Kennedy on foreign aid issues and how the expensive, often touchy political matter of economic foreign policy would play in Middle America during the 1960 campaign. By offering carefully arranged data and optimistic forecasts, Reuss helped Kennedy avoid overly vague speeches on the Third World and economic aid. He recommended a continuation of "first step" rhetoric, combined with elusive promises to "use the right key" in order to win the cold war by 1970.[36]

The other Democratic presidential hopefuls for 1960 failed to see any political pluses in the idea of changing cold war tactics. Senator Lyndon Johnson (D-Texas), the Senate majority leader, saw no reason to revise American foreign policy and predicted that Soviet bumbling in the 1960s would have greater influence on events than State Department soul searching. Hubert Humphrey saw the call for new foreign policy approaches as overly alarmist and said that the issue required careful study. Adlai Stevenson, musing over a third run at the presidency, complained that Kennedy's "Ugly American" echoings were pure "Hollywood," for they ignored the significance of the United Nations' role in assisting the Third World. The United Nations, he said, continued to be discarded as a solution to Third World dilemmas. A grander financial and philosophical commitment to it would be the real "right key." Stuart Symington, meanwhile, continued to draw fire for political foolishness over his foreign service cadet corps idea, and Senator Henry "Scoop" Jackson (D-Wash.) worried that America's military posture might be adversely altered thanks to the new attention on economic and moral measures.[37]

Despite these comments and concerns, it was Kennedy's comparison of *The Ugly American* appeal to Harriet Beecher Stowe's one hundred-year-old *Uncle Tom's Cabin* that won the biggest spotlight. America was at a crossroads, he explained. Like one century earlier, the United States faced a great contest. This time, it was communism versus anticommunism not North versus South. America, he stressed, had had the strength to survive the Civil War thanks to the determination of a powerful presidency. It required that presidency again to rescue the Third World and win the cold war.[38] Without question, this type of rhetoric separated Kennedy from the rest of the Democratic presidential crowd, but that was not good enough. Since 1956 he had had the credentials to draw press and public attention. Capitalizing on his *Profiles in Courage* publicity and on an internal Democratic party report concerning Catholic disaffection with the Eisenhower administration, Kennedy had pursued the 1956 Democratic vice presidential nomination after the party's convention had opened the vote to its delegates.

Given the account of his old attractions to McCarthyism, his high absentee record, and lack of interest for the procedural work of the Senate, Kennedy's move was a daring one. He hoped that his decision would be seen within the rising *Profiles in Courage* image of a World War II hero with much in common with some of America's great historical figures. Being handsome and telegenic aided his efforts, but the party turned to its New Deal vanguard in the person of Senator Estes Kefauver of Tennessee. Taught never to accept defeat by his father, Kennedy took the loss as a severe personal blow. His staff, on the other hand, quickly regrouped, comparing Kennedy's defeat to Lincoln's 1858 loss to Senator Stephen Douglas and to Franklin Roosevelt's defeat in 1920 while serving as the party's vice presidential candidate.[39] Both Lincoln and Roosevelt became better men because of these traumas, even Kennedy soon concluded, and the door opened wider to the presidency.

Now considered daring and courageous for having challenged the older deans of the Democratic party, and with an attractive rhetorical flair to boot, Kennedy hoped that Massachusetts, and especially the nation, was ready for his new, more liberal side. He needed a cause, and one that would neither divide opinion nor keep it preoccupied too long. Jousting against French elitism and stupidity, even more so than he had in 1954, provided him that temporary, headline-grabbing cause. He attacked France, a NATO ally, on the Senate floor for its Algeria policy. More than a French colony, Algeria had been a department of France since the 1830s. Witnessing an increasingly violent movement for Algerian independence since the fall of French Vietnam in 1954, the French government considered the Algerian rebels communist-influenced. The French tried to convince the Eisenhower administration that these rebels had much in common with the communist Viet Minh of the 1946–1954 Vietnam War.

Eisenhower had little comment on the matter, but Kennedy said the French were disguising a classic case of nineteenth century-style colonial conflict as an anticommunist cause. Only a few years earlier, Kennedy had condemned France's Vietnam policy in a little noticed, trial balloon-styled speech. Now, with cameras rolling, he lambasted Eisenhower for considering the Algerian matter an "internal French problem." Freedom and independence he announced, had long been America's concern.[40]

Kennedy's new notoriety and positive publicity translated into a 875,000 landslide vote margin over his 1958 Senate rival, Vincent Celeste. It was his state's largest landslide ever, and the nation's most successful Senate race in 1958.[41] His foundation for a presidential bid was especially solid. Yet, his foreign policy platform remained incomplete. Would his newly professed interest in the cold war fortunes of the Third World, coupled to his vague promises of America triumphant over any communist challenge, be strong enough to win a presidency? Change was both attractive and dangerous to the American voter. Which would it be in 1960? He needed a foreign policy proposal that kept his innovations alive, but recognized the concerns of the old cold warriors and a still conservative America.

The literary, academic world continued to provide Kennedy with enough innovations to attract an interested press and voting public. Kennedy himself had never been a scholarly man, but his parents had insisted on tireless self-improvement exercises. A healthy respect for intellectual achievement wedded to the desire for personal growth was part of the Kennedy psyche.[42] Hence, he had no objection to borrowing the ideas of Sorensen, Lederer and Burdick, and others, for he enjoyed the possibility of someday turning those ideas into policy. They also presented the possibility of continuing his preferred style of "new ideas" campaigning, which, if handled properly, could be used effectively against the so-called "tired" old men of the Eisenhower White House. In 1960, he found new blood in Dr. Walt Rostow who helped him bridge the gap from "new ideas" to a successful campaign.

Soon to be one of Kennedy's most important foreign policy advisors, Professor Rostow of M.I.T. published *Stages of Economic Growth: A Non-Communist Manifesto* in early 1960. The work had been influenced by popular press reports and think tank analyses that predicted a Soviet economic boom within a few years. By the mid-1960s, some predicted, Soviet industrialization and the resulting economic indicators would overshadow United States productivity and economic policies. Rostow's research confirmed the trend, and he urged the American political community to deal with the Soviet Union as if it were a business competitor. To demonstrate America's competitive spirit, he recommended an expanding space program, new missile systems, a high technology military in general, and a new commitment to even greater domestic economic growth.[43]

Rostow's work offered Kennedy the incentive to rail against America's "missile gap" arsenal in contrast to the Soviet Union, as well as speak in favor of a "modernized military." These comments were consistent with his call for better schools to compete against Soviet scholarship and with the "get America moving again" theme of his campaign. In terms of crisis management, Rostow favored quick military responses to new Soviet threats in the world.

Although the future president found him arrogant in tone and personality, Kennedy welcomed Rostow in his inner circle. His ideas, put in the format of the Kennedy campaign, were comforting to arch cold warriors and to the generally conservative voter who found it intriguing to consider the Soviets businesslike rivals.[44] The written word had once again influenced Kennedy's campaign game plan; however, the place of foreign policy in his campaign waned as that campaign proceeded.

To John Kennedy, and especially to his brother and cautious campaign manager, Robert, moving to the political center meant staying away from the divisive issues of foreign policy. Beyond the basic themes of the "new ideas" politics culled from *Profiles in Courage*, *The Ugly American*, and *Stages of Economic Growth*, little was said unless necessary. Hubert Humphrey, Kennedy's principal rival in the early 1960 presidential primaries, helped define that necessity, especially during the April 1960 Wisconsin primary. Humphrey depicted himself as the soul of the Democratic party, a tireless defender of the rights of labor and an advocate of civil rights reform as early as the 1948 Democratic National Convention. In the area of foreign affairs, Humphrey remained vague and most uninspiring. Despite his talk of pulling the party together, Humphrey insisted that unnamed party members should "return to reason" in foreign policy. He promised to "rally all Americans" in an undefined great crusade against communism. The implication of Humphrey's remarks was that Kennedy had been too close to the McCarthy point of view, and, therefore, divorced from "reason." He also implied that Kennedy lacked any sense of vision concerning the direction of American foreign policy, possessing only a few alleged "new ideas."[45]

Humphrey accented his message in Wisconsin where he had been known as "Wisconsin's other senator" during the early- and mid-1950s McCarthy era. The label meant that Humphrey had stood for decent, moderate politics in nearby Minnesota while McCarthy had turned a once Progressive and liberal state into a haven for right-wing Republicanism. Humphrey hoped to capitalize on his positive image in Wisconsin, link Kennedy to McCarthy, and jump-start his own steamroller to the nomination. Yet, McCarthy had suffered a vote of censure in the Senate several years earlier and had died in 1957. Wisconsin's political memories proved to be short.

With both Kennedy and Humphrey claiming the same loud allegiance to organized labor, urbanization, and civil rights, only foreign affairs promised to separate the two candidates and tip the scales to victory.

With his old friend and advisor, Congressman Henry Reuss, at his side, Kennedy delivered a self-proclaimed major address on foreign policy at Milwaukee's Serb Hall shortly before the Wisconsin vote. An important gathering place for Wisconsin labor activists and Democratic party stalwarts, Serb Hall was an excellent location. It was also an excellent opportunity to look more presidential than Humphrey. The latter preferred outdoor rallies with backslapping comrades and an informal press-the-flesh style. Kennedy remained ill at ease "politicking with the boys," and generally preferred the great solitary speech where the spotlight shone on him alone. Hence, he delivered his major address, attacking the missile gap, favoring the high technology military, as well as stressing his Third World concerns and cold war victory determination. A vigorous foreign policy, he said, was a good investment for the nation.

Although it avoided specifics, Kennedy's Serb Hall address was a rousing one. It pulled together all of Kennedy's major themes on a 1960s foreign policy. *The Milwaukee Journal*, the state's largest daily and proud of its Democratic party bias, praised the speech and shifted its support from Humphrey to Kennedy. The paper's editors still could not pinpoint their attraction to Kennedy's foreign policy; they just concluded that it "sounded" new and exciting. Humphrey, they believed, had not done enough homework on foreign affairs and was beginning to take the Wisconsin voter for granted. The Wisconsin voter apparently agreed with this sentiment, for Kennedy won a sizable majority in their state.[46]

Humphrey later complained that Wisconsin's crossover primary tradition led Republican voters to the Kennedy camp, thereby dooming the Humphrey campaign. Big money from the Kennedy family was also involved in contrast to Humphrey's collection of modest donations. The *Caroline*, Kennedy's private campaign plane, helped the candidate reach the small towns of Wisconsin's rugged north country, and Robert Kennedy did his best to mobilize the Catholic vote, even if it meant sending anti-Catholic hate mail to Catholic voters. But Kennedy remembered his victory there as America's first-time recognition of his foreign policy.[47] It also gave him a frontrunner position.

Given the frenetic nature of primary campaigning, and Kennedy's grassroots style, the foreign policy platform of the Kennedy campaign never fully developed. In May 1960, during the West Virginia primary, he stressed quality of life issues and the disparity between rich and poor.

He touted his heroism in World War II and the friendships he made in the Pacific with common men. Thus, he avoided anti-rich boy charges in a poor state. Meanwhile, he denounced anti-Catholic bigotry as often as possible, implying that his opponents were desperate and ready and willing to level anti-Catholic slurs against him. They were not. Kennedy won more than 60 of the vote in West Virginia, and nothing was said of foreign policy. His opposition folded, although Adlai Stevenson tried another comeback at the Democratic National Convention. Kennedy remained assured a first ballot victory, and Stevenson urged him to consider the continuing importance of the United Nations when discussing foreign affairs during his nomination speech. Despite these urgings to embrace specifics, Kennedy spoke only vaguely of a New Frontier, whereby America could accomplish most anything in the world arena through determination, strength, and national commitment.[48]

NEW FRONTIER

This basic thesis came from yet another published political tome, Guy Emerson's *New Frontier*. Published in 1920, Emerson's work supported an interventionist, pro-Woodrow Wilson America in the face of the growing post-World War I attraction to isolationism. America's success abroad, Emerson wrote, required the involvement of Americans from all walks of life. Isolationism would lead to the destruction of democracy at home and in Europe, he predicted.[49] Like the Emerson he had once read in the family library and at Harvard, Kennedy alluded to foreign policy in vague, yet grandiose terms during the last months of the campaign. America's special mission, special purpose was noted, along with the usual foreign policy concerns that he had finally pulled together back in Wisconsin. Even the Emerson-inspired "ask not what your country can do for you, but what you can do for your country" would not emerge until the inaugural.

As the 1960 campaign proceeded, the gap between the public and the private Kennedy widened. In foreign affairs, this meant Kennedy continued to appeal to a public opinion which supported vigorous new tactics in anticommunism. It also meant that he doubted his own rhetoric. Following his nomination, Kennedy hoped to establish a foreign policy "brain trust" in the interest of fleshing out these new anticommunist tactics. Supposedly modeled off FDR's anti-Great Depression "brain trust" of the 1932–1933 interregnum, the Kennedy foreign policy group was expected to include the nation's finest young Democratic party experts in international relations. Although originally formed to assist in the latter weeks of the campaign, the group never formally organized itself until after the Kennedy election. Most of its members had had campaign, academic, or business commitments, and Kennedy later complained that he could have used their specific advice against Richard Nixon in the televised Nixon-Kennedy debates of October 1960.[50]

In confidential communication with this always fluctuating group, Kennedy told veteran diplomat and foreign policy analyst Chester Bowles, Arthur Schlesinger, and others that "revolutionary turmoil lost China, not Truman" and that America could not lure poor nations away from communist attractions. His private comments reflected more pessimism than vigor, and he hoped that he was wrong. Or, so he said.[51] These pessimistic observations dominated his private thoughts on foreign affairs during the late summer weeks of the 1960 campaign when he trailed Vice President Nixon in the polls.

At the time of his nomination, Kennedy expected Nixon to defend the Eisenhower record in foreign affairs, making it easy for him to link the two with "tired policies." His expectations proved wrong. Nixon understood the appeal of Kennedy's "new ideas" campaign and tried his hand at it himself to the great annoyance of the Kennedy team. Nixon never spoke specifically of "missile gaps," Third World "relief," and cold war "victory." Instead, he spoke of keeping the peace that Eisenhower had maintained, avoiding the "bellicose tone" in foreign policy that Kennedy's "vague promises" embraced, and providing a 1960s foreign policy built on the experience of a vice president who had been actively involved in special missions abroad and policy making at home.[52] In the long run, Nixon's appeal of youth plus experience in foreign affairs was as vague and as carefully crafted as Kennedy's; however, he still remained linked to the "tired old men." As long as Kennedy stressed that point, he always had the political ear of the country. This did not mean, of course, that he had to like the situation. Kennedy had planned on an opponent who was simply a younger version of Eisenhower and with limited political talents. Nixon never accommodated.

Privately Kennedy denounced Nixon as a "philandering politician who operated on a wing and a prayer."[53] Many Democrats held the same view, but the voting public wondered if Nixon had not changed from the days when he was the House of Representatives' tamer version of Senator Joe McCarthy. He now appeared more mature, i.e., more presidential. He no longer blamed America's foreign policy problems on an internal subversion conspiracy that had been instigated by FDR's New Deal. Eisenhower had even continued, if not expanded, the New Deal's interventionist mission in American life through developments such as Health, Education, and Welfare (HEW) and the St. Lawrence Seaway project. Nixon had been there to reap the bipartisan support for these measures in between official tours to Latin America and Europe. Moreover, Kennedy could not even attack the vice president on the easy ground of representing the party of Herbert Hoover and Great Depression economic miseries. The economy was still healthy, in spite of enduring recession. Nixon dodged labels and it troubled the Kennedy team.[54] It helped to explain Kennedy's frustrating denunciation of the vice president as the "wing and a prayer" candidate.

Kennedy's frustration level reached an all-time high when an autumn opinion poll suggested that a majority of Americans saw his foreign policy ideas as "weak." Nixon provided both stability and determination, the poll pointed out, and Kennedy remained an intriguing but unknown factor. Kennedy's shocked advisors were divided on how to handle this new problem, while Kennedy himself bemoaned the fact that his foreign policy brain trust remained scattered across the country.[55] Time was running out. The four-part televised debate with Nixon promised to be something of the preamble for the general election, for the first Tuesday in November was only days away.

Arthur Schlesinger worried that the American people might not be sophisticated enough to accept his boss's "new ideas" on foreign policy. A tiring Kennedy agreed, but he also worried if his doubts on cold war "victory" and related issues were showing. Robert Kennedy assured him that that was not the case. In the television debates, Robert advised his brother, the major objective would be simple: "make the other guy look more tired than you." Consequently, talk of "Ugly Americans" or "Profiles in Courage" would be avoided in the debates, for highbrow foreign policy discussions would bore the audience as well as present a certain staid, professional look. Instead, Kennedy would bring foreign policy back to the anticommunist basics, such as attacking the Eisenhower administration for permitting the rise of Fidel Castro's communist Cuba. Tough talk might submarine the "weakness" issue, or so the Kennedy team hoped. That approach, combined with a decent telegenic performance, could turn the tide against Nixon.[56] It did.

Although most radio listeners thought Nixon did a fine job in the debates, television viewers saw in Kennedy a reincarnation of one of the Democratic party's best orators, William Jennings Bryan, and one who exhibited the determination of a Franklin Roosevelt circa 1932. It was a series of black-and-white images that voters remembered, not substance. Nixon's five-o'clock shadow, perspiration, and nervous gulps from his complimentary water glass were suddenly serious liabilities. Meanwhile, Eisenhower's predebate comments on the shooting down of an American U-2 mission over Soviet territory were mediocre, non-committal, and on the minds of television viewers. Kennedy offered an eloquent dose of strident anticommunism on the U-2 issue which contrasted greatly to Eisenhower's "something has to be done" statements. Kennedy had no specific plan either, but he successfully linked Nixon to the alleged mediocrity of the Eisenhower presidency. The link was made easier to build thanks to Eisenhower himself, who, shortly before the debates, offered the poorly timed admission that his vice president had played a smaller role in foreign policy making than he thought. The president's comments were in reference to the general role of any vice president, and Kennedy shared Eisenhower's assessment of that limited role.[57] Nevertheless, it aided the image of the vigorous Kennedy versus the tired braggart, Nixon.

Be it lingering concern over Kennedy's Catholicism, youth, inexperience, comfort with Eisenhower conservatism, or all of the above, Kennedy's record-slim popular vote over Nixon had little to do with foreign policy posturing. Was Schlesinger right? Did America lack the intellectual gifts to digest the Kennedy message on foreign affairs? Was that message good enough, and what direction did it need to take? Whereas Kennedy had once perceived foreign affairs to be his strong point, the electorate had apparently disagreed. It troubled him, and he asked the brain trust to come up with a working foreign policy agenda by Christmas 1960.

In the closing days of the campaign, Kennedy had made five speeches on foreign affairs in contrast to two apiece on race relations and the economy. During December 1960, the undersecretary of state-designate, Chester Bowles, and the secretary of state-designate, Dean Rusk, told Kennedy that his stress on academic-styled theses, culled from interesting books, had been the wrong way to present a foreign policy. The American people, they said, would have preferred a point-by-point agenda. Their comments implied that the American people were not necessarily dumb, just confused.

Rusk, a Georgia moderate and State Department career official, believed that the first plank of a Kennedy foreign policy required the reaffirmation of strong presidential authority and full respect for the principle of executive privilege. Eisenhower, and even Truman to an extent, had been too lax in delegating their authority over national security policy and foreign affairs in general. They permitted Joe McCarthy to steal the show or allowed the secretary of state to define most aspects of foreign policy. Rusk volunteered that he would be happy to "serve" the president. Never would he interfere with a presidential decision. America's best foreign policies were built by powerful presidents, and the two Roosevelts were seen as the finest role models for this century. Rusk's brain trust colleagues agreed with his conclusions. Kennedy, in turn, welcomed their recommendation. Yet, he worried that his incoming staff, known for their youthful enthusiasm and intellectual curiosity, were too willing to say "Yes sir" and avoid analytical advice. It was contradictory, but he wanted both.[58]

Bowles, Burns, and Schlesinger believed that the American people at least got the drift of Kennedy's message on Third World issues and cold war victory. Hence, the new administration's basic concerns in foreign affairs did not need to be altered. Kennedy's brain trust advisor, supported by Senators Jackson and Fulbright, agreed that in European affairs America offered "confusion and lack of leadership." In Asia, the Eisenhower administration had "been equally inconsistent, and often dangerously doctrinaire," while problems in Africa and Latin America had "been largely ignored." Their conclusions on how to meet these challenges were less vague than during the campaign period; however, fundamental objectives continued to remain more attractive than specifics. "There is not only an urgent need," Kennedy was advised, "but a clear public commitment for a fresh approach to foreign policy in most areas of the world and the refocusing of American energies and influence in dealing with other nations.[59]

One of the best ways to "refocus energies" would be to reform the entire Foreign Service within the first Kennedy year in the Oval Office. Bowles and Rusk especially favored this approach. The McCarthy era, they believed, had had a devastating effect on America's international affairs bureaucracy. McCarthy's "Red baiting" had either led to the firing of competent Foreign Service officers or led to their early retirement in favor of business and academe. The State Department, Bowles stressed, was filled with sycophants and do-nothings who labeled all innovative ideas as radical anti-Americanism. Dean Rusk went even further, railing against the strong possibility of anti-Kennedy sabotage on the part of the Eisenhower leftovers. Lyndon Johnson, the former Senate majority leader and now vice president-elect, worried that the legislative assistants on Capitol Hill who specialized in foreign affairs had been attracted to government service by McCarthy tactics and by the very visible success of McCarthy's senior legislative assistant, Roy Cohen. He too feared sabotage and called for quick but undefined reforms. Senator Henry "Scoop" Jackson simply recommended firing them all.[60]

Kennedy himself hoped to surround his office with the "best and brightest" minds in foreign affairs, i.e., fortyish Harvard graduates with an attraction to government service and the Democratic party. Those "best and brightest," nevertheless, insisted that their advice would be meaningless unless the presidency somehow increased its powers in order to negate the Eisenhower leftovers factor. Meanwhile, top-to-bottom personnel reviews would lead to an easier path for the Kennedy foreign policy.

Yet the Kennedy foreign policy remained elusive throughout the Eisenhower lame duck period. Despite good intentions and mounds of well-written position papers, the usual lip service to the "Ugly American" and "vigorous leadership" themes was made. This did not mean that the Kennedy team was avoiding a 1961 agenda in foreign affairs. They simply could not agree on one. America, on the other hand, did not have to know about these troubles. The public was told to expect great changes and dramatic innovations in the conduct of foreign affairs, deliberately raising positive images of FDR's activist New Deal and World War II victory.[61]

Popular memory, over a generation later, prefers to keep the Kennedy-FDR image intact. Benjamin Bradlee, the early 1960s editor-in-chief of The Washington Post and a Kennedy supporter, had admitted "guilt" in helping to spread, if not create, this image. He complains that the press for "the first and last time" had been smitten by a smooth-talking president-elect. Kennedy's foreign policy plans were dangerously hollow, Bradley remembers, and no one really cared.[62] Before the inaugural, the press and the public were more intrigued by Kennedy's youth and flamboyance, not the mechanics of foreign policy.

Kennedy and his advisors at least agreed on basic directions in foreign affairs preceding the inaugural. First of all, the largest danger to any foreign policy-building effort was seen as the political right and not the left. That was obvious from the Kennedy team's concern over lingering McCarthyism. They also saw an alleged 25 percent of their own party, the liberals, as a nuisance. Adlai Stevenson was deemed their leader, and the nuisance was defined as undue respect for the United Nations as well as a certain tiredness in challenging communism at any place, any time. The nuisance could be overcome, Kennedy believed, for Democratic party liberals had nowhere else to turn but to him. On the other hand, since they still constituted much of the activist heart of the party, concessions had to be made. Stevenson would be sent to the United Nations as United States ambassador, for instance. He could be forgotten there, Kennedy concluded, and the liberals would think the appointment was an honor.[63]

If the United Nations was ineffective and a dumping ground for American political liabilities, then winning the cold war required full unilateral commitments. Of course, the victory march did not have to look unilateral, especially since the Third World respected the United Nations. If the cold war in the 1960s was truly to be won or lost in the Asian/Pacific region first, as Kennedy's "Ugly American" comments always implied, then a new effective international organization, run by America behind the scenes, would make the job easier. Although they had no catchy name for it in late 1960, this new organization (called New Pacific Community by mid-1961) would be headquartered in Australia to avoid "Ugly American" charges, consist of delegates from the entire Asian/Pacific region, and arrange infrastructure improvements projects for themselves. America would maintain a low key but big budget presence there, attempt to isolate China and the nonaligned states as too radical and too poor to assist in Third World development, and slowly win the complete allegiance of the Asian/Pacific Third World to the American position in the cold war. It all required careful political craftsmanship and Kennedy enjoyed talking about that challenge with his "best and brightest" colleagues.[64]

By mid-January 1961, Kennedy's foreign policy agenda continued to remain in the realm of a stock political speech. There were plenty of dreams and he expressed them eloquently in his inaugural address; however, his "pay any price, bear any burden" theme remained a rehash of both the Truman Doctrine and his own campaign rhetoric. The problem of finding a working foreign policy to match the win the cold war promise was a fundamental one. It was linked to the possibility of world nuclear destruction in order to achieve it, and, therefore, it was always politically expedient to avoid specifics about it. Kennedy played the game well, but it continued to produce a number of contradictions. Several Kennedys had indeed emerged by late January 1961 and it would be difficult for him to combine their characteristics into one successful foreign policy-maker. There was the radical Kennedy, i.e., the eloquent speechmaker attracted to the politics of commitment and vigor. There was the New Deal Kennedy, promising a rebirth of FDR-styled activism. There was the moderate Kennedy, always concerned about the cost of the cold war and whether middle America really wanted an expanding economic foreign policy or lower taxes at home. There was the conservative Kennedy. The latter worried that members of his own party favored cooperation rather than confrontation with the Soviets. Finally, there was the intellectual Kennedy who wondered if cooperation was not better than confrontation, if World War III was not inevitable, and if America really needed a Messiah-like president who had all the answers.

The American electorate did not see this confusion in January 1961. They saw inspiration, elegance, a great promise of things to come. People wanted to respond to Kennedy's call to "do for your country," and they did. The Peace Corps, the Alliance for Progress, and even the Special Forces would please them, but Cuba, Berlin, and especially Vietnam would soon haunt them. The legend of Camelot, Kennedy's most concrete accomplishment, was about to be built. His foreign policy endeavors played a key role in that legend.

ENDNOTES

1. Theodore Sorensen quoted in "JFK: His Vision, Then and Now," *U.S. News and World Report*, October 24, 1988, p. 33.
2. Assassination anniversary statement for the *Congressional Record*, November 22, 1984 by Representative Mervyn Dymally (D-Calif.), personal files.
3. Thomas Cronin, "On the American Presidency: A Conversation with James MacGregor Burns," *Presidential Studies Quarterly* (Vol. XVI, No. 3), Summer 1986, pp. 528–542; Arthur M. Schlesinger, Jr., *The Cycles of American History* (Boston, 1986), p. 405.
4. For a study of the intellectual and political influences on the young John Kennedy, see: Joan and Clay Blair, *The Search for JFK* (New York, 1976) and Herbert Parmet, *Jack: The Struggles of John F. Kennedy* (New York, 1980). For the 1960 campaign-era opinion of Burns and Schlesinger, see

James MacGregor Burns, *John Kennedy: A Political Profile* (New York, 1960), and Arthur Schlesinger, *Kennedy or Nixon? Does It Make Any Difference?* (New York: 1960).

5. Kennedy's wavering between liberal and conservative role models is a major concern of David Burner and Thomas R. West, *The Torch is Passed: The Kennedy Brothers and American Liberalism* (New York, 1985).
6. Kenneth W. Thompson, "Kennedy's Foreign Policy: Activism versus Pragmatism," in Paul Harper and Joann P. Krieg, eds., *John F. Kennedy: The Promise Revisited* (New York, 1988), pp.25–34; James MacGregor Burns, *The Power to Lead* (New York, 1984), p. 75.
7. Office of Naval Intelligence/FBI Report, August 1942, Personal Papers of JFK, JFK Library; Robert A. Divine, "The Education of John F. Kennedy," in Frank Merli and Theodore A. Wilson, eds., *Makers of American Diplomacy* (New York, 1974), pp. 317–343.
8. Kennedy to his parents, September 12, 1943, Personal Papers of JFK, JFK Library.
9. See the extensive account of the 1946 campaign and aftermath in the preface to U.S. Congress, *John F. Kennedy: A Compilation of Statements and Speeches Made during His Service in the United States Senate and House of Representatives* (Washington, 1964).
10. *Ibid.*, Vol. 1
11. Richard Whalen, *The Founding Father* (New York, 1964), p. 419; Charles Bartlett, "John F. Kennedy: The Man," in Kenneth W. Thompson, ed., *The Kennedy Presidency* (Lanham, MD, 1985), p. 3.
12. *Ibid.* The most analytical work on the political relationship between young John Kennedy and his father remains David Koskoff, *Joseph P. Kennedy* (Englewood Cliffs, NJ, 1974).
13. Lessons and Legacies," a compilation of statements and press clippings on the 1952 campaign by the staff of Senator John F. Kennedy, January 1953, Papers of Senator John F. Kennedy, JFK Library.
14. *Ibid.* Walter Johnson, ed., *The Papers of Adlai E. Stevenson*, Vol. 6 (Boston, 1976), pp. 283–284.
15. Reminiscences of September 12, 1953 (wedding of John Kennedy and Jacqueline Bouvier), Personal Papers of John F. Kennedy, JFK Library; Peter Collier and David Horowitz, *The Kennedys* (New York, 1984), p. 197; Doris Kearns Goodwin, *The Fitzgeralds and The Kennedys* (New York, 1987), pp. 769–774.
16. John Buchan was also a friend of the Kennedy family. His ideas on Democratic politics included maintaining a proper image for national leaders, i.e., projecting but not necessarily embracing strong family values. See Buchan's "Tribute to the Kennedys" (1920), Personal Papers of John Kennedy, JFK Library; and John Buchan, *Pilgrim's Way* (New York, 1920).
17. Southeast Asia Tour Files, Spring 1954, Papers of Senator John F. Kennedy, JFK Library.
18. Parmet, *The Struggles*, p. 285.
19. Kitty Kelley, *Jackie Oh!* (Secaucus, NJ, 1978), pp. 30, 51.

20. Quotations of Eleanor Roosevelt, Box 1 of the Biographical Files of the Papers of Eleanor Roosevelt, Franklin D. Roosevelt Library. For background on Mrs. Roosevelt's interest in both diplomacy and activism, see: Timothy Maga, "Humanism and Peace: Eleanor Roosevelt's Mission to the Pacific, August-September, 1943," *The Maryland Historian*, Vol. XIX, No. 2 (Fall/Winter 1988), pp. 33–47; and Blanche Wiesen Cook, "Turn Toward Peace: Eleanor Roosevelt and Foreign Affairs" in Joan Hoff Wilson and Marjorie Lightman, eds., *Without Precedent: The Life and Career of Eleanor Roosevelt* (Bloomington, 1984), pp. 108–121.

21. Kennedy's attraction to dominance over both women and nations is pondered at length by Garry Wills, *The Kennedy Imprisonment: A Meditation on Power* (Boston, 1982), p. 31.

22. John W. Ward, *Red, White and Blue: Men, Books, and Ideas in American Culture* (New York, 1969), p. 148; Theodore C. Sorensen, *Kennedy* (New York, 1965), pp. 68–70

23. Correspondence between Office of Senator Gary Hart (D-Col.) and author, September 1984 (personal files). See also: Susan Berry Casey, *Hart and Soul.* (Concord, 1986), p. 299.

24. Compare the opening chapter of Kennedy's *Profiles in Courage* (New York, 1956) to Mary W. M. Hargreaves, *The Presidency of John Quincy Adams* (Lawrence, KS, 1985). The latter presents an Adams more concerned about practical government than the former.

25. Speeches, "Sputnik" file (1957), Papers of Senator John F. Kennedy, JFK Library.

26. Burns, *Kennedy*, p. 125; Sorensen, *Kennedy*, pp. 65–66.

27. Speeches, "The United States and Mankind" (1959), Papers of Senator John F. Kennedy, JFK Library.

28. "The Ugly American," *The Nation*, October 4, 1958, p. 199; "The Ugly American," *The Saturday Evening Post*, November 8, 1958, p. 4.

29. See the introduction to William Lederer and Eugene Burdick, *The Ugly American* (New York, 1960).

30. Whereas Fulbright and Symington remained the most vocal on the alleged "Ugly American problem," both Democratic and Republican Senators rushed to have their official comments on this "problem" placed in the *Congressional Record* of early 1959. See: U.S. Congress, Senate, *The American Overseas. Hearings Before the Committee on Foreign Relations*, 86th Congress, 1st Session (Washington, D.C., 1959).

31. Lederer and Burdick, *The Ugly American*, p. 122.

32. H. W. Brands, Jr. *Cold Warriors: Eisenhower's Generation and American Foreign Policy* (New York, 1988), p. 211; Richard A. Melanson and David Mayers, eds., *Reevaluating Eisenhower: American Foreign Policy in the 1950s* (Urbana, 1987). Melanson and Mayers find Eisenhower more in control of foreign policy than Kennedy believed, and that the former also had strong, but privately held, ideas on Third World relations and cold war victory.

33. Joseph Buttinger, "Fact and Fiction on Foreign Aid: A Critique of 'The Ugly American' " *Dissent, A Quarterly of Socialist Opinion*, Vol. 6 (Summer 1959), pp. 319–320.
34. Lederer and Burdick, *The Ugly American*, pp. 166, 233.
35. Robert A. Parkenham, *Liberal American and the Third World* (Princeton, NJ, 1973), pp. 20–21; Arthur Schlesinger, *Robert Kennedy and His Times* (Boston, 1978), p. 440.
36. Reuss was part of a growing and nicknamed "Wisconsin Mafia" of young Kennedy activists in 1959 and early 1960 who hoped that their chosen candidate could clinch the nomination by mid-primary season and the strategically important Wisconsin primary. See Reuss's correspondence with fellow Wisconsin Kennedy activist, governor of the state, and soon to be Senator (1962), Gaylord Nelson, Archives of the State Historical Society of Wisconsin.
37. See the Senate Hearings on *The American Overseas*; U.S. Congress, Senate, *Mutual Security Act of 1959, Hearings Before the Committee on Foreign Relations*, 86th Congress, 1st Session (Washington, DC, 1959–1960).
38. Excerpts from the Campaign Speeches of Senator John F. Kennedy (1960), Papers of Senator John F. Kennedy, JFK Library.
39. Burns, *Kennedy*, p. 190.
40. Press clipping: *New York Times*, July 3, 1957, p. 1, Speeches of Senator John F. Kennedy, JFK Library; Ronald Nurse, "Critic of Colonialism: JFK and Algerian Independence," *The Historian*, Vol. 39 (February 1977), pp. 307–326.
41. David Burner, *John F. Kennedy and a New Generation* (Glenview, IL, 1988), p. 35.
42. Lawrence O'Brien, *No Final Victories* (New York, 1974), p. 2.
43. Walt Rostow, *Stages of Economic Growth: A Non-Communist Manifesto* (New York, 1974), p. 2.
44. Rostow's influence and ideas are reviewed briefly in a National Security Council Memorandum to Kennedy, "An Effective Countertheme to 'Peaceful Coexistence,' " July 14, 1961, Box 52/Classified Subjects–NSC, The Papers of Theodore Sorensen, JFK Library.
45. Theodore H. White, *The Making of the President, 1960* (New York, 1967), p. 94; Pierre Salinger, *With Kennedy* (Garden City, NY, 1966), p. 34; Kenneth O'Donnell and David F. Powers, *"Johnny, We Hardly Knew Ye"* (Boston, 1970), p. 160; See the Humphrey campaign/Wisconsin (1960) file in the bulging collection of campaign material in the Pre-Presidential Papers of John F. Kennedy, JFK Library.
46. *Ibid.* See also the small, but valuable Milwaukee Country/Wisconsin Primary (1960) collection, including material contributed by Representative Henry Reuss and Representative Clement Zablocki (D-South Milwaukee), at the Milwaukee County Historical Society. Hubert H. Humphrey, *Education of a Public Man* (Garden City, NY, 1976), p. 248.
47. Sorensen, *Kennedy*, pp. 133–138.

48. Lawrence Fuchs, *John F. Kennedy and American Catholicism* (New York, 1967), pp. 176–177; "Nomination Test," *The Washington Post*, September 13, 1960, p. A16.

49. Guy Emerson, *The New Frontier* (New York, 1920).

50. For detail on the brain trust, an account of their views and relationship to Kennedy, see the lengthy memorandum on "Considerations Regarding the Selection of Top Policy Makers," Chester Bowles to Dean Rusk, December 18, 1960, Box WH-3a/Chester Bowles of the Papers of Arthur M. Schlesinger, Jr., JFK Library.

51. *Ibid.*

52. White, *Making of the President*, p. 337. Nixon's rhetoric, current analysts suggest, might have been the result of growing disgust in the Eisenhower administration for Cold War extremism. See: Anthony Clark Arend, *Pursuing a Just and Durable Peace: John Foster Dulles and International Organization* (New York, 1988), p. 135.

53. "Considerations Regarding the Selection of Top :Policy Makers," December 18, 1960, Box WH-3a/Chester Bowles, Papers of Arthur M. Schlesinger, Jr., JFK Library.

54. Walt Rostow, *The Diffusion of Power* (New York, 1972), p. 296.

55. Chester Bowles, *Promises to Keep* (New York, 1971), Part III.

56. Allen J. Matusow, *The Unraveling of America: A History of Liberalism in the 1960s* (New York, 1984), p. 31; Austin Ranney, *Channels of Power: The Impact of Television on American Politics* (New York, 1983), Chapters 5 and 6.

57. John F. Kennedy, "If the Soviets Control Space—They Can Control Earth," *Missiles and Rockets*, Vol. VII (October, 1960), pp. 12–13, JFK Library; J. Richard Snyder, ed., *John F. Kennedy: Person, Policy, Presidency* (Wilmington, DE, 1988), pp. 11–24.

58. Dean Rusk, "Reflections on Foreign Policy" in Kenneth Thompson, ed., *Kennedy Presidency*, pp. 190–201; "Considerations Regarding the Selection of Top Policy-Makers," December 18, 1960, Box WH-3a/Chester Bowles, Papers of Arthur M. Schlesinger, Jr., JFK Library.

59. *Ibid.*

60. *Ibid.*

61. The opening chapter of Montague Kern, Patricia W. Levering, and Ralph B. Levering, *The Kennedy Crises: The Press, the Presidency, and Foreign Policy* (Chapel Hill, NC, 1983).

62. Benjamin Bradlee to Peter Jennings in ABC-News Documentary *JFK Remembered* (November, 1983).

63. See the Stevenson chapter in Seymour Maxwell Finger, *Your Man at the UN: People, Politics, and Bureaucracy in Making Foreign Policy* (New York, 1980).

64. Secretary of State Rusk to Kennedy, February 2, 1961, and Kennedy's "New Pacific" (Speech in Hawaii, August 1960), POF/Box 111 and Senate Files, JFK Library.

CHAPTER 2

The Cuban Crises and the Alliance for Progress: A Lesson in National Self-interest

As early as 1961, a certain yardstick could have been applied to the American electorate's support for foreign policy adventurism, but Kennedy either preferred to ignore it or accept only part of it. America would support high-intensity conflicts for short periods, or low intensity conflicts for long periods, but not high-intensity conflicts for long periods. Unless the interests of the United States were obviously threatened, it was the viability of the confrontation that mattered. This lesson was never mastered by Kennedy, although he was given an early taste of its implications in the Bay of Pigs crisis and again in the Cuban missile crisis.

"Let every nation know," Kennedy announced in his inaugural address, "that we shall pay any price, bear any burden, meet any hardship, support any friend, oppose any foe to assure the survival and the success of liberty."[1] On April 17, 1961, as Cuban exiles waded onto the beaches of the Bay of Pigs, Kennedy faced his first crisis in his young presidency. He stood firm on his invasion decision, but then decided to leash American air support for the anti-Communist rebels. Fidel Castro defeated them quickly. This might have been the harsh lesson concerning the application of rhetoric to reality; however, the "can do" White House of the early 1960s saw it as a temporary setback. More vigorous anticommunist endeavors were now required elsewhere.[2]

Like an admiral or general, the commander-in-chief is often forced to fight the last war yet another time. As he spoke it, Kennedy's "bear any burden" promise was already outdated in military terms. The young president's call to activism continued to remain influenced by the legacies of World War II, the world of Guadalcanal and inevitable American triumph. With a dash of romance, he appealed to a generation eager to rule over themselves. Yet, Kennedy's conclusion that Eisenhower's foreign policy was tired, worn, and too passive did not reflect his otherwise strong attraction to analytical conclusions. Eisenhower ruled a nation that painfully adjusted its politics and economics following both World War II and Korea. It was also a nation that worried over the possibility of nuclear war stimulated by overly aggressive White House policies. What Kennedy saw as Eisenhower passivity was, in reality, the first sign that American power had limits and that its influence in the world was fading. Despite Kennedy's interest in first signs and steps, he preferred to cloud this reality and it still won him political support.

There were new rules of war when Kennedy launched the Bay of Pigs invasion. He failed to acknowledge them as well. The new rules were not written at Tarawa or Saipan, but at the North Korea–China border when General Douglas MacArthur was refused permission to advance into China. In an era of "police actions," demilitarized zones, and weapons too horrible to use, the suggestion of "bearing any burden" made little sense. All of this constrained American policy to accept the limits of its own national self-interest. It would take two crises over Cuba, and a struggling, idealistic Alliance for Progress to Cuba's neighbors, to acquaint Kennedy with this point.

Embracing the lessons of hard-nosed reality would always negate the great promises of Kennedy's inaugural address and vote-attracting image. Hence, he could only partially accept the politics of self-interest. Nevertheless, in late October 1962, he admitted to the nation that his administration-long battle with Fidel Castro, and now with Moscow over its nuclear support of Castro's defense, "was a fight over U.S. national security, not over the spread of Communism in the hemisphere."[3] Kennedy's Cuba policy made it clear that he would "pay any price" to maintain America's basic interests in hemispheric defense, and the Soviets truly learned that fact. In the meantime, Kennedy would not apply what he learned about national self-interest in Cuban matters to other areas of policy. Southeast Asia became his new "bear any burden" symbol, and the promise of the New Frontier continued on the other side of the globe.

BAY OF PIGS

Kennedy's education on the significance of national self-interest in foreign policy had had its roots in the so-called "passive" Eisenhower administration considerations for a Bay of Pigs invasion. Viewed as tottering and experimental by the Eisenhower White House, Castro's new regime in Havana would fall, the Central Intelligence Agency predicted, if assaulted by American-supported Cuban rebels. Also predicting that Castro's attraction to Marxist-Leninism would lead to a formalized Soviet satellite status for Cuba, the Central Intelligence Agency (CIA) claimed that the Soviets could win the cold war in the western hemisphere by making a mockery of America's flagging influence in the region. There was no alternative to quick military action, they concluded, and massive American air cover would guarantee success.[4]

Eisenhower had requested the CIA's study in the early spring of 1960. Three arch cold warriors, all of them holdovers to the Kennedy presidency, had devised the innocently titled "Cuban Program." The three were Allen Dulles, director of the CIA; Richard Bissell, deputy director of the CIA; and General Lyman Lemnitzer, chairman of the Joint Chiefs of Staff. Bissell had been in charge of the Cuban Program, but Dulles and Lemnitzer would become the chief advisors to President-elect Kennedy concerning the program. Bissell was strongly interested in the military mechanics of the plan, especially air cover. Dulles and Lemnitzer were more concerned about its urgent political necessity, making sure that the new, young president understood the power that Castro might soon wield over Latin American opinion. Cuba, they insisted, was a four-letter word and the race for cold war victory in the western hemisphere was now in high gear. They found a receptive audience in Kennedy and his staff. Youth and inexperience did not mean a lack of commitment to cold war adventurism. Apparently, the CIA had discounted Kennedy's foreign policy comments as just stock speech rhetoric. They were mistaken.

Given his enthusiasm, wild sense of humor, and tireless Kennedyesque energy, Tracy Barnes of the CIA worked the Kennedy cabinet and staff most effectively. Stressing that the "Cuban Program" was not a "real part of the Republican past," but "living within the cadence of the New Frontier," Barnes predicted that military success in Cuba would lead to respect for American determination in Southeast Asia and elsewhere. Barnes's only problem in winning the full commitment of the new Kennedy White House regarded conflicting reports of CIA activity already in Cuba. Arthur Schlesinger complained that the CIA was America's worst enemy in the "Cuban Program." Undercover CIA agents in Cuba had told certain individuals that American ownership of pre-Castro era properties would be restored after the invasion. Hence, anti-Castro guerilla activities in Cuba would eventually lead that guerilla into a postwar American job near his home. Schlesinger thought this type of CIA promise played into Castro's attacks on American economic imperialism in Cuba, and he was right. Even Kennedy agreed that such matters would lose "hearts and minds" even before the invasion was launched, but it did not deter his decision to support the "Cuban Program."[6]

Less than six days into the new Kennedy administration, the president had approved the invasion plan. There were plenty of questions over the competence of the CIA-trained personnel, the precise motives of the Cuban exiles involved, and the stress on air cover. Kennedy was particularly concerned about the latter, for the invasion's success depended on its appearance as a Cuban-led liberation campaign. Meanwhile, the competence questions and his own intellectual instincts made him "wary and reserved," in his own words, to the plan.[7] Nevertheless, a launch date was set, and he remained opposed to air cover support. America would not be "bearing any burden" at the Bay of Pigs. Barnes tried to assure the Kennedy team that their worries were unfounded, for the Cubans would welcome the liberators at the time of the invasion. The Kennedy team wanted to believe that Barnes was correct, and, by the end of March 1961, they had convinced themselves that the New Frontier version of cold war retaliation required this response.[8]

Convinced or not, Kennedy felt committed to follow through New Frontier rhetoric accordingly. There was little alternative to invasion. Executed during the early morning hours of Monday, April 17, 1961, the invasion had become a total disaster within its first moments. Air cover was never provided and the last units of the Cuban exile brigade were captured on Wednesday, April 19, 1961. Blaming "gaps in intelligence plus some errors in ship loading, timing, and tactics," Kennedy, nevertheless, took "full responsibility" for the invasion's quick failure. Hoping for a tolerant America, Kennedy turned to his favorite medium, television, and lectured the nation on these responsibilities. His speech was similar in tone to an address made by his archrival, Richard Nixon, several years earlier. Nixon, facing charges of questionable political behavior, had made a televised address (Checkers Speech), burying the questions at hand and accenting his patriotic service to the nation. Although more terse and withdrawn than his usual self, or even than the less telegenic Nixon, Kennedy, like the Nixon of the early 1950s, asked the electorate for a second chance. Suggesting that great policies lay ahead, he said that victory in the cold war was still America's destiny. Few Americans heard defeat in the president's words, and most, according to the resulting public opinion polls, were happy to continue their support for this determined young president.[9]

In contrast to his two beleaguered successors during the height of the Vietnam War, Kennedy got off easy in the realm of public opinion. The Bay of Pigs, unlike Vietnam, had been a fast moving affair and the public appreciated Kennedy's candor concerning its failure. Because of that continuing public support, Kennedy found it easy to relegate the episode to "poor planning" and turn to other cold war tasks. There was little soul searching and few position papers written concerning what the Bay of Pigs might mean for U.S.-Cuban-Soviet relations. Arthur Schlesinger, often derided by Kennedy as the "in-house intellectual," and aide, McGeorge Bundy, always concerned about the decision-making process and how to improve it, offered their advice to Kennedy on the subject. Yet, most of the Kennedy team followed Secretary of State Rusk's lead. Rusk saw an urgent nature in the march to cold war victory and saw little need to rehash the administration's stumble into the Bay of Pigs disaster. The Cuban exiles, he stressed, had never had a "snowball's chance in hell."[10] Their defeat was their own, not Kennedy's. C'est la vie.

In any event, during the next several months, various lessons would be recognized by Kennedy. There was no requirement to translate a lesson into policy, however. Kennedy recognized that point as well. Whether they liked it or not, the Kennedy team would be familiarized with basic Bay of Pigs—related questions, such as the need for better communications between government agencies, the need for full allied consultation and adherence to international law, and the need for developing a coordinated and manageable decision-making style during times of crisis.

Throughout the Bay of Pigs operation, communications had been poor. The National Security Council had divorced itself from the mechanics of the plan, leaving the details to the CIA in the field. Consequently, they were of little use to the president as close advisors on the "Cuban Program." Meanwhile, the lack of air cover was seen as a temporary Kennedy decision in some government agencies and not in others. The White House did nothing to confirm or quash these rumors, leading some CIA agents and anti-Castro Cubans to conclude that Kennedy had abandoned them in a ruthless, quickly made "reversal" of an air cover decision. Although newspaper accounts, British intelligence, and the State Department reported on the strength of Castro's forces and political popularity, the CIA offered an exact opposite portrait and worked hard to keep non-CIA reports out of Kennedy' s hands. For all effective purposes, Kennedy had permitted himself to use only one source of information, the CIA.[11] He would return to his analytical self during the Cuban missile crisis. His comfortableness in ignoring analysis in April 1961, even though his heart was never committed to military adventurism in Cuba, can only be explained via inexperience and the early "can do" euphoria of the New Frontier.

During the building of the "Cuban Program" and its implementation, both the Latin American capitals and the European allies were ignored. Neither their advice nor concerns were requested. An unflattering view of an invasion of Cuba was therefore avoided, for the allies, the New Frontiersman believed (and particularly in the opening months of the administration), were tangential to cold war victory plans.[12] This arrogance would only foster anti-American sentiment in Latin America toward Kennedy's Alliance for Progress economic assistance goals, and it would trouble the European allies' sense of worth in global affairs. Moreover, although a moral case might have been made to support a Cuban exile invasion of Cuba, there was no justification within the guidelines of international law. Indeed, Kennedy preferred to avoid the issue of moral and international justification altogether, and kept his public praises for the Cuban exile community in south Florida to a minimum. He preferred the support of the United Nations in American–Third World relations, and he would solicit their support in the coming Cuban missile crisis.[13]

There had always been a stark contrast between what Kennedy thought he had been coordinating versus the reality of the Bay of Pigs. He believed that the Cuban exiles were "quietly reinfiltrating" their country, whereas, in fact, the invasion had been prepublicized and exaggerated to Normandy-landing proportions. Kennedy thought the exiles understood the limited U.S. support for their adventure. Hence, he was surprised at the resulting "Kennedy sellout" argument by the defeated invaders. Finally, the CIA assured Kennedy that the Bay of Pigs region was a guerilla fighter's dream. In reality, it was a swamp, well-defended by Castro's forces, and the exiles were ill-trained to handle the situation.[14]

Kennedy was to say later that his new administration had not been "fully organized for crisis management" by April 1961. The president's advisors said "yes as one voice" on the invasion decision, even though the U.S. military had serious reservations and Robert Amory, the CIA's deputy director for Intelligence, had not been informed of the "Cuban Program."[15] Amory's office was viewed as too analytical by the "Cuban Program" architects, thereby lacking courage and commitment to daring cold war plans. Meanwhile, Robert Kennedy and Theodore Sorensen, two of the president's closest and most trusted advisors, were left out of the invasion decision process. Usually, Kennedy preferred to ask "impolite and tough questions" of his staff before proceeding with a decision. The "Cuban Program" engineers implied that analytical government was against the interests of cold war victory, reminding Kennedy of his "bear any burden, pay any price" rhetoric.[16] At the Bay of Pigs, Kennedy, as his father had taught him, did "not shrink from adversity," but he also had failed. Moreover, he had failed without weighing variables or alternatives, an unacceptable approach to his father as well. After April 1961, he intended on managing the crisis rather than becoming part of it. On the other hand, he still felt electorate-bound to his militant cold war rhetoric and to the Alliance for Progress, the Latin American policy he had announced prior to the Bay of Pigs. This dilemma would haunt him for the rest of his administration.

ALLIANCE FOR PROGRESS

The Kennedy cabinet, and Kennedy himself, were introspective enough to look back on the Bay of Pigs as "an overdose of vigor" and laughed at the problem. They also offered no comfort to Castro. John McCone, Kennedy's choice to succeed Allen Dulles after the Bay of Pigs, supervised sabotage and commando raids into Cuba under the code name of Operation Mongoose. There was even talk of assassinating Castro, but, as in so many areas of Kennedy policy making, talk rarely meant policy.[17] The policy for Cuba's neighbors and all of Latin America remained the Alliance for Progress. That policy's commitment to economic growth and humanitarian concern oddly balanced the vengeful approach to Cuba.

Echoing Franklin Roosevelt's Good Neighbor promises of the early 1930s, Kennedy had campaigned in 1960 for a Latin America that would establish an economic infrastructure strong enough to support thriving democratic governments from Chile to Mexico. The image of the "Ugly American," who supported dictatorship over reformist politics, thrived more than any economy in Latin America. Kennedy had denounced that image, promising quick remedies once elected. Those remedies, he believed, would also deaden the appeal of Castro to the downtrodden.[18] Consequently, the Bay of Pigs threatened to intensify "Ugly American" images in Latin America and offset the political inroads made via massive U.S. economic aid. Those threats would never loom as large as Kennedy feared; however, the Alliance for Progress remained Kennedy's best foot forward toward Latin America throughout his administration.[19]

Expected to reverse economic decline, initiate dozens of infrastructure assistance plans, remedy problems in land and tax policy, and provide expertise in the areas of health and education, the Alliance for Progress promised to amass a $10 billion treasury, with full Latin American consultation. The Alliance project, announced in Uruguay just weeks after Kennedy's inauguration, was outlined in even more eloquent terms than usual by the young president.

Representing one of the largest debtor nations in Latin America, the Brazilian government had, at first, doubted a new U.S. commitment to economic rescue plans south of the American border. Kennedy's answer to Brazil was typical of the glowing rhetoric applied to the Alliance for Progress hope.

The Alliance for Progress represents the response of free peoples to the problems of our times. Like Tiradentes and Jefferson, who helped forge the political philosophy of the New World, we are given the opportunity to set economic and social goals whereby the age-old specters of fear, want, disease, and ignorance can be overcome. Together then, let us press forward under this Alliance and meet these challenges so that our peoples can enjoy that full incasure of Order and Progress for which Brazil and the United States are so well known and for which we both can be justly proud.[20]

❬ Kennedy's populist-styled rhetoric on behalf of the Alliance was well received in Latin America. Meanwhile, the Alliance project itself was an adequate match for Castro's rebel appeal within Washington's battle for "hearts and minds" in Latin America. The region's economic decline was halted. Low income housing provided by Latin American governments eliminated inhumane living conditions for thousands and quelled revolutionary sentiment. Basic educational benefits, provided within the new housing projects, assaulted illiteracy. Health care became more accessible to the impoverished. Real progress was made, and it could be already witnessed by 1963.[21]

On the other hand, Kennedy's rhetoric, promising an "economic revolution where democracy can bloom" suggested more than a handful of improvements in select areas. It suggested the redistribution of wealth, the collapse of right-wing dictatorship in favor of democracy, and a new era of economic growth for all classes of Latin American society.[22] Since the Kennedy administration also favored the political stability of anticommunist regimes in the effort to keep communists out of power, the above suggestions remained impossible to achieve❭ The rhetoric did not match the performance, and policy-making contradictions assured limited results. Nevertheless, a certain onus was on the Latin American governments as well. The formula for success required the active participation of the Alliance partners. Adlai Stevenson, Kennedy's U.N. ambassador, reported in July 1961 that the Alliance was welcome in a variety of Latin American states, but it was sometimes viewed as "El Plan Kennedy" or a unilateral handout effort. During March 1962, Kennedy reminded the Latin American governments that the Alliance required nations working together with Washington:

No matter what contribution the United States may make, the ultimate responsibility for success lies with the developing nation itself. . . . Only you can eliminate the evils of destructive inflation, chronic trade imbal-

ances and widespread unemployment. Without determined efforts on your
part to establish these conditions for reform and development, no amount
of outside help can do the job.[23]

Kennedy had been warned by his own State Department against high
hopes for the Alliance. Arturo Morales-Carrion, the deputy assistant
secretary of state for inter-American affairs, even told Kennedy that the
project was too idealistic and wasteful. Moreover, he pointed out that
the State Department's Foreign Service officers (FSOs) in Latin America
felt the same way and probably opposed the project with greater vehe-
mence than he. The FSOs, Morales-Carrion insisted, were a "tightly-
knit club" who considered the Kennedy White House a meddler in the
status quo of U.S.-Latin American relations. They also saw the Alliance
as an invitation to political collapse, the rise of the liberal left, and
chaos. Thus, Kennedy could expect only a modicum of support from
his arch-conservative representatives on-site in Latin America.[24]

The FSO matter reminded Kennedy of Chester Bowles's old predictions of policy sabotage by lingering Eisenhower bureaucrats. He fired
off a series of angry notes to the diplomatic corps in Latin America
during mid to late 1961, and mobilized his brother, the attorney general,
and Arthur Schlesinger. The latter individuals were sent to Latin America to preach the New Frontier to America's own embassy personnel,
rather than to Latin American governments. Although the reasoning
behind it eluded him, the president had been told that Robert Kennedy
and Schlesinger enjoyed more respect in the eyes of the FSOs than he.[25]
This mission to Latin America was reasonably successful, but Morales-
Carrion remained correct on the overly idealistic objectives of the Alliance.

Convincing Congress of America's destiny vis-à-vis the Alliance for
Progress also was not as easy as originally assumed. Eisenhower had
once recommended long-term Congressional authorization of Third
World development loans. His Congress had agreed in a certain bipartisan spirit, and the then Senator Kennedy had participated in the effort.[26] In both 1961 and 1962 the House voted against these loans, and
always at a time when the Kennedy administration was about to conclude a new loans deal with the Latin Americans. With the anger and
determination of an outraged anticommunist, Kennedy publicly berated
the House for failing to "meet its responsibilities and halt the spread
of Communism and Castroism by every available means."[27] They reversed their vote as requested, but it was apparent that Congress's en-

thusiasm for a Marshall Plan-like mission to Latin America was not as strong as the Marshall Plan era of the late 1940s and early 1950s.

Kennedy was aware of the idealistic nature of the program, yet still expected practical results. In October 1961, the member nations of the Alliance agreed on paper to the "principle" that the success of the Alliance depended on their own level of participation. The "principle" implied a commitment to the ethical use of U.S. assistance funds. That commitment remained elusive and by 1963 it became a matter of personal concern and frustration for Kennedy.[28]

Despite glowing promises to improve upon the infrastructure of their country, the military junta in charge of Peru used funds earmarked for domestic economic recovery and reform to assure their political power base. They increased the military budget by 33 percent in one year and tripled the salaries of the officer corps. Over $18 million was targeted to purchase twelve RB-57 bombers, and the Peruvian embassy in Washington managed to gather a petition, countersigned by several Republican congressmen, justifying military over economic reform expenditures as vital to the cold war.

The purpose of the petition involved heading off any Kennedy protest of Peruvian misuse of funds, for that protest would make the American president look less anticommunist. Peruvian cleverness or not, political liability or not, Kennedy still protested the Peruvian approach, making further arms deals a difficult affair for the junta.[29] This did not end the misuse issue, nor further exploitation of America's interest in anticommunist priorities; however, Kennedy's toleration of recipient abuse and exploitation of American generosity had worn thin before his November 1963 assassination.[30] Yet, he left behind no recommendation for a change in tactics or policy. Cold war caution and pragmatism prevailed.

CUBAN MISSILE CRISIS

One important reason for Kennedy's ever-growing interest in peaceful U.S.-Latin American relations involved the political fallout from the Cuban missile crisis of October 1962. Following that crisis, Kennedy's pro-Alliance rhetoric became even more glowing and embraced a sense of urgency. With America's national security safeguarded through his handling of affairs in October 1962, his opposition to nuclear war solutions grew more profound and his concern for hemispheric and world peace grew in proportion.[31]

The opening developments of the 1962 version of Kennedy's ongoing Cuban problem evolved during a tense congressional election campaign. Although Kennedy had been granted his "second chance" from the electorate after the Bay of Pigs, the Republican party had every intention of reminding the voter how bankrupt that "second chance" had become. Kennedy, for instance, had sent a diplomatic mission to Havana urging the release of Bay of Pigs invaders, but the mission failed to win an agreement. This difficulty, coupled with the fact that Kennedy appeared powerless to halt growing Soviet influence in Cuban internal and military affairs, had become a significant part of the Republican campaign assault on the White House.[32]

Labeled a champion of the politics of inaction by the Republican opposition, Kennedy admitted he had no idea what the Soviets were planning for Cuba in 1962. He just hoped the Soviets would respect America's longstanding hemispheric interests, dating back to the Monroe Doctrine of the 1820s, and avoid any challenges to the American-maintained balance of power.[33]

Overtaken by civil rights matters, Berlin, and Southeast Asia, Cuba had disappeared from the headlines until the summer of 1962. Both *The New York Times* and *The Washington Post* reported a buildup of Soviet armaments in Cuba. By the first days of October 1962, there were daily reports on the topic, fueling the Republican charge of Kennedy "inaction." Shortly before its campaign recess, the Senate, in a move led by pro-Kennedy Democrats, voted 86–1 in favor of using "massive retaliation" against Cuba should the growing U.S.S.R.-Cuba connection lead to communist expansionist efforts in the western hemisphere. The Soviets replied with a declaration of their own, noting that an American attack on Cuba would be considered an American attack on Soviet territory.[34] Helping Kennedy beat back the Republican assault, the Senate Democrats did nothing to lessen Soviet-American tensions. Hence, those tensions were at a high level even before the formal beginning of the missile crisis in mid-October 1962.

Neither the Republican nor the Soviet assault on Kennedy waned in mid-October 1962. New York's avowed liberal Republican senator, Jacob Javits, said he supported much of the president's idealistic agenda, but that he feared Kennedy "lacked the courage" to invade Cuba. Senator Homer Capehart, an avowed Republican conservative from Indiana, wanted the White House to announce a precise timetable for invasion. There could be no turning back from war, he concluded. In the press, syndicated columnist and sympathetic New Frontiersman, James Reston, attacked the Republican warmongering as irresponsible and unnecessary, yet urged Kennedy to demonstrate leadership by informing the American people about the level of Soviet military involvement in Cuba.[35]

⟨While the Republicans and the press debated the possibility of war, the presence of Soviet offensive missiles in Cuba was not yet known to the Kennedy White House. The U-2 photographs of the missile silos would be studied by the cabinet on October 16, 1962, following two weeks of sword-rattling by arch cold warriors who had stressed fear, rumor, and partisan politics. The mid-October issue of *Newsweek* assailed Kennedy's Cuban policy, urging action against Castro's military buildup program and calling Kennedy a "profile in indecision." The president answered his critics, warning that he would respond to any threat that challenged American national self-interest: "If at any time the communist build-up in Cuba endangers our security in any way we will do whatever must be done to protect our security and that of our allies."[36]⟩

In the realm of rumor, the most circulated talk in mid-October involved a secret deal to reduce the American presence in Berlin in exchange for a reduced Soviet presence in Cuba. Secretary of State Rusk denounced the rumor, but, with the congressional elections looming and a sizable percentage of Democrats finding the rumor attractive, Rusk also noted that Khrushchev and Kennedy would be ready to discuss such a deal after the upcoming holidays. In the realm of partisan politics, former President Eisenhower attacked Kennedy and Ambassador Stevenson at the U.N. as do-nothings in the face of communism, explaining that the White House planned to recognize Castro after the November elections. Kennedy could quote the Gallup Poll which said that 60 percent of the nation opposed a war over Cuba, or *Newsweek* which claimed 90 percent opposition.[37] A certain political standoff had been reached, for these same polls indicated majority support for some sort of action.

⟨Kennedy could survive this standoff, and resolve the crisis at the same time, if he found the proper compromising technique. On October 16 and 17, the Kennedy cabinet met to find that technique, and Robert Kennedy set the tone by opposing any "Pearl Harbor in reverse." McNamara supported him.[38] Meanwhile, previously scheduled appointments were kept to present a normal business day image to the press.

By the weekend of October 20–21, Kennedy was beginning to receive positive press for his "careful" handling of Cuban affairs, and *The Washington Post* accused the Republicans of running against Castro and not Kennedy. With that development, Kennedy urged the nation's major publishers to be equally as "careful" in reporting Cuban-related news, at least until America's allies were fully informed of Washington's position on escalating Soviet support for Castro. Since the president was expected to offer this information in a major television address on October 22, the publishers reluctantly agreed. Benjamin Bradlee of *The Washington Post* represented the primary voice behind the media muzzle. A staunch Kennedy supporter who regarded himself as within the president's inner circle, Bradlee later regretted the precedent that was established here; however, Kennedy did announce a naval blockade ("quarantine") over Cuba as scheduled.[39]

Kennedy had urged his cabinet to consider five alternatives: (1) no action, (2) action through political and diplomatic channels, (3) a surgical air strike, (4) an invasion, (5) a blockade. Isolated by much of the cabinet as too soft on communism, Ambassador Stevenson at the U.N. was also labeled as too slow moving for the American people and too accommodating to Soviet defense plans in Cuba. His "mobilize U.N. efforts" idea met blank stares. The leadership of the Senate Foreign Relations and House Foreign Affairs Committees favored invasion or, in compromise, at surgical air strike. The National Security Council favored military action as well, and the more discussion on the topic the more the Kennedy brothers saw naval blockade and vigorous U.N.-based diplomacy as the best policy.[40]

Insisting that Americans were ready to pay "the cost of freedom," the president had helped establish a scenario for World War III. With the collapse of the stock market, the raids on grocery markets for "fall-out-safe" foods, and the general depressed state of the nation, Kennedy would learn that the electorate was not ready to "bear any burden." At the same time, Kennedy's "missile gap" campaign politics came back to haunt him, for U.S. missiles remained in place near the Turkish-Soviet border. The president's approach implied that the New Frontier could have it all, i.e., successful prosecution of the Monroe Doctrine in "America's hemisphere" and the Truman Doctrine fully enforced as well.

With Kennedy standing firm on the blockade decision, and with a Cuba-Turkey missile swap considered appeasement, Premier Khrushchev began to use diplomatic channels to issue even more condemnations of the all-powerful America versus tiny Cuba.[41] By October 24, Castro's new missiles were reaching operational status, and Kennedy made it clear to Khrushchev that the United States was ready for war. U-Thant, the U.N. secretary general, urged that both sides reassess their positions before it was too late. Although Kennedy and Khrushchev scoffed at the reassessment idea in their official responses, Khrushchev ordered cargo ships entering the blockade zone to stall, and Kennedy began to turn more seriously toward using the good offices of the U.N..[42]

With the press still debating a Cuba-Turkey missile swap and analyzing Kennedy's responsibility for the crisis, the White House still entertained air strike and invasion options. Khrushchev rescued the Kennedy team from escalating the matter with a promise to dismantle the missiles if America promised not to invade. Yet, within twenty-four hours he added the proviso of American withdrawal of the missiles in Turkey. Treating Khrushchev's approach as two separate policy statements, as well as ignoring information regarding an American U-2 plane shot down over Cuba, the White House responded to the earlier Soviet proposal and issued a "no invasion" guarantee. The crisis was defused and Kennedy announced to a relieved electorate that there were no victors in the events of October 1962, only "survivors."[43]

Kennedy's final epitaph for the missile crisis best reflected the mood of the nation, and the voters would reward the party of their modest president in the congressional elections of early November. Ex-President Eisenhower, championing a new anti-Kennedy tack in the twilight of the congressional campaign, charged that the young president had manufactured much of the crisis to assure Democratic party voter support in the election. Kennedy personally found the charge distasteful, given the hard reality of the near-World War III situation. Nevertheless, more than twenty years later, historians would be leveling similar charges.[44]

For Kennedy and his elite band of New Frontiersmen, the missile crisis became a great test of inaugural address idealism and 1960 campaign promises. The effort to win the cold war around the world could also destroy it, Kennedy had warned his audience and himself, but the warning was usually discarded in favor of the ambitious, "can do" philosophy that towered over it. The desolate streets of America during the missile crisis surprised Kennedy. Instead of frightening Americans into their homes, the crisis was supposed to rally Americans into an anticommunist solidarity, or so Kennedy had originally assumed. Fear, hope, and progress for peace were more common expressions in the electorate than cries for invasion or nuclear war.

All of this continued to be a revelation to Kennedy, who, like his staff, had chosen to become isolated within their own New Frontier political promises. Hence, Kennedy, who had fostered the largest peacetime arms race in his nation's history, now sought "first steps" toward nuclear disarmament and favored a ban on nuclear tests in the atmosphere.[45] As always, "first step" politics, when eloquently spoken and now combined with the modest "survivors" image of the Cuban missile crisis, promised Kennedy the electorate's favor. Within a year, he would succeed in this endeavor, suggesting that Kennedy and the American people worked best together when the White House labored for peace and not cold war victory.

Be it the Bay of Pigs, the building of the Alliance for Progress, or the Cuban missile crisis, the Kennedy administration operated with a basic assumption, i.e., that American foreign policy was a defensive mechanism and that the Soviets were the aggressor. The Soviets maintained the same assumption, but from a reversed position. Like Woodrow Wilson during the First World War, Kennedy saw his policies as a means to "end all wars." Eventually, both he and his Soviet counterpart recognized the fact that this approach could also end all of civilization.

In the end, Kennedy responded to communist threats in the western hemisphere within a policy that best benefited American survival and Monroe Doctrine-related self-interests. Kennedy's rhetoric and the reality of anticommunist politics still made it difficult for the president to abandon cold war political axioms. Moreover, there is no evidence to suggest that he preferred to do so, outside of frustrated comments to his family and aides against the "politics as usual."[46] The Truman Doctrine continued, and so did the New Frontier commitments to it. Meanwhile, the "pay any price" thesis could be demonstrated well in a Third World setting where threats of nuclear war remained remote. The cold war recoiled from nuclear options after the Cuban crisis, but that development offered little solace to the many Third World residents who became the new center stage of cold war confrontation.

ENDNOTES

1. For the writing of the inaugural address and its impact on Kennedy idealism, see the opening material to Theodore C. Sorensen, *Kennedy* (New York, 1963), pp. 68–70.
2. State Department Memorandum: "Responsibility for the Bay of Pigs," September 1961, WH-6, Papers of Arthur M. Schlesinger, JFK Library.
3. "Political and Military Responses to Current Soviet Initiatives," Position Paper for the "Agenda for Executive Committee Meeting," October 27, 1962, Box 49/Classified Subjects, Papers of Theodore Sorensen, JFK Library.
4. Stephen E. Ambrose, *Eisenhower the President* (New York, 1984), pp. 24–28. R. Gordon Hoxie, *Command Decisions and the Presidency: A Study in National Security Policy and Organization* (New York, 1977), p. 243.
5. "Cuban White Paper," March 25, 1961, WH-6, Papers of Arthur M. Schlesinger, JFK Library.
6. *Ibid.* "Sordid Examples of U.S. Government Policy," July 29, 1961, WH-6, Papers of Arthur M. Schlesinger, JFK Library.
7. *Ibid.* Peter Wyden, *Bay of Pigs: The Untold Story* (New York, 1979), p. 310. See also the introduction to Richard Welch, *Response to Revolution: The United States and the Cuban Revolution, 1959–61* (Chapel Hill, 1985). Thomas G. Paterson, "Fixation With Cuba," in *Kennedy's Quest for Victory*, pp. 123–155.
8. "Cuban White Paper," March 25, 1961, WH-6, Papers of Arthur M. Schlesinger, JFK Library. Donald Ritchie, ed., *Executive Sessions of the U.S. Senate Foreign Relations Committee, 1961*, Vol. XIII, Part 1, (Washington, D.C., 1984), Bay of Pigs Hearings.
9. Montague Kern, Patricia W. Levering, and Ralph B. Levering, *The Kennedy Crises: The Press, the Presidency, and Foreign Policy* (Chapel Hill, 1983), pp. 3–24.
10. Schlesinger, *A Thousand Days*, pp. 224, 252–256; Roger Hilsman, *To Move a Nation*, pp. 32, 78; Warren I. Cohen, *Dean Rusk* (Totowa, NJ, 1980), pp. 96–115; "Political and Military Responses to Current Soviet Initiatives," Position Paper for "Agenda for Executive Committee Meeting," October 27, 1962, Box 49/Classified Subjects, Papers of Theodore Sorensen, JFK Library.
11. Hoxie, *Command Decisions*, pp. 330, 335–336.
12. "What Framework of Settlement Would be Satisfactory to the United States?," Position Paper for "Agenda for Executive Committee Meeting," October 27, 1962, Box 49/Classified Subjects, Papers of Theodore Sorensen, JFK Library.
13. Kenneth W. Thompson, "Kennedy's Foreign Policy: Activism versus Pragmatism," in Paul Harper and Joann P. Krieg, *John F. Kennedy: The Promise Revisited* (New York, 1988), p. 32.
14. Memo on the CIA and the Bay of Pigs, Schlesinger to Kennedy, July 29, 1961, WH-3a/CIA, Papers of Arthur Schlesinger, JFK Library.

15. *Ibid.*
16. See the conclusion to Trumbull Higgins, *The Perfect Failure: Kennedy, Eisenhower, and the CIA at the Bay of Pigs* (New York, 1987).
17. Schlesinger, *A Thousand Days*, p. 227; Irving Janis, *Groupthink: Psychological Studies of Policy Decisions and Fiascoes* (Boston, 1982), Chapter 2.
18. Simon G. Hanson, *Dollar Diplomacy Modern Style: Chapters in the Failure of the Alliance for Progress* (Washington, D.C., 1970), pp. 1–16; R. Harrison Wagner, *United States Policy Toward Latin America* (Stanford, CA, 1970), p. 41.
19. Kennedy speech to Latin American diplomats, White House, March 12, 1962. WH-2/Alliance for Progress, Papers of Arthur Schlesinger, JFK Library.
20. "Formulation of the Alliance for Progress" in "Actions to Build Friendships and Strengthen Ties in Latin America," January–July 1961, and McGeorge Bundy to Kennedy, February 21, 1962, Box 34/Subject Files, 1961–64: Foreign Policy, Papers of Theodore Sorensen and Box 290/Alliance for Progress, 1/62–3/61, NSF-Subjects, JFK Library.
21. Teodore Moscoso, U.S. Coordinator, Alliance for Progress, to Kennedy: "Country and Program Developments," February 15, 1963, Box 291/Alliance for Progress, 1/63–4/63, NSF-Subjects, JFK Library.
22. Graham Martin, Acting U.S. Coordinator, Alliance for Progress, to Kennedy, November 9, 1962, WH-2/Alliance for Progress, Papers of Arthur Schlesinger, JFK Library.
23. U.S. Embassy-LaPaz to Secretary of State Rusk, March 15, 1962, and Kennedy to Latin American diplomats, March 13, 1962, *Ibid.*
24. Schlesinger to Kennedy: Memo on the Bureau of Inter-American Affairs, June 27, 1961, WH-2/Alliance for Progress, Papers of Arthur Schlesinger, JFK Library.
25. *Ibid.*, and Bi-Weekly Reports, Office of the Coordinator, Alliance for Progress, July-September 1961, *ibid.*
26. Stephen G. Rabe, *Eisenhower and Latin America: The Foreign Policy of Anti-Communism* (Chapel Hill, 1988), pp. 134–152; Dwight Eisenhower, *The White House Years*, Vol. II, *Waging Peace, 1956–1961* (Garden City, NY, 1965), p. 539.
27. Kennedy to Congress, August 16, 1961, Box 49, POF, JFK Library.
28. Bi-Weekly Report, Office of the Coordinator, Alliance for Progress, October 1961 and "Problems in Alliance for Progress," November 12, 1963, WH-2/Alliance for Progress, Papers of Arthur Schlesinger, JFK Library.
29. Teodore Moscoso, U.S. Coordinator, Alliance for Progress, to Kennedy: Memorandum on "Peru Junta's Resource Allocation Questioned," February 15, 1963, Box 291, NSF-Subjects/Alliance for Progress.
30. "Program Developments of November," Moscoso to President Lyndon Johnson, November 30, 1963, *ibid.*
31. Morton H. Halperin, *Nuclear Fallacy: Dispelling the Myth of Nuclear Strategy* (Cambridge, MA, 1987), pp. 15–21; John Lewis Gaddis, *Strategies of Containment* (New York, 1982), pp. 198–236.

32. The influence of domestic American politics on the Kennedy administration's handling of Cuban affairs is a primary research effort of Professor Thomas Paterson at the University of Connecticut-Storrs. He finds a strong influence and considers it an unfortunate development in the conduct of diplomacy and the chances for peace. One of Paterson's finest investigations remains "October Missiles and November Elections: The Cuban Missile Crisis and American Politics, 1962," *Journal of American History*, Vol. 73, No. 1 (June 1986), pp. 87–119.

33. Ambassador Adlai Stevenson to Kennedy, October 27, 1962, Box 49/Classified Subjects, Papers of Theodore Sorensen, JFK Library.

34. See "The Missile Crisis: The National Clandestine Phase" in William J. Medland, *The Cuban Missile Crisis of 1962: Needless or Necessary?* (New York, 1988).

35. Kennedy began to weigh the advice of experts and political luminaries on October 16, 1962 (which is generally regarded as the first day of the crisis). The John F. Kennedy Library maintains an extensive collection of Cuban Missile Crisis-related material. In analyzing the Kennedy decision process, one of the more valuable collections involves the transcripts of the Executive Committee of the National Security Council (ExCom). ExCom met twice on October 16, 1962 and a variety of proposals, criticisms, and alternatives were discussed.

36. "International Law Problems of Blockade," Department of State Legal Memorandum to McGeorge Bundy, September 10, 1962; Sorensen Memo: "Attempts to Equate Soviet Missile Bases in Cuba with NATO Jupiter Bases in Italy and Turkey," and Kennedy to Sorensen, October 16, 1962, Box 49/Classified Subjects: Cuba, Papers of Theodore Sorensen, JFK Library.

37. Alexander George and Richard Swake, *Deterrence in American Foreign Policy, Theory and Practice* (New York, 1974), pp. 466–491; Desmond Ball, *Politics and Force Levels* (Berkeley, 1980), pp. 88–104.

38. Arthur Schlesinger, *Robert F. Kennedy and His Times* (Boston, 1978), pp. 524–555; Robert F. Kennedy, *Thirteen Days* (New York, 1969), p. 31.

39. James Nathan, "The Missile Crisis: His Finest Hour Now," *World Politics*, Vol. 27 (January, 1975), p. 263; Paul Anderson, "Decision-Making by Objection and the Cuban Missile Crisis," *Administration Quarterly*, Vol. 28 (June, 1983), pp. 201–222.

40. NSC Executive Committee Record of Action, October 25 and 27, 1962, Meetings No. 5 and 7, Box 52/Classified Subjects: NSC, Papers of Theodore Sorensen, JFK Library.

41. National Security Action Memorandum No. 200 and "Acceleration of Civil Defense Activities," October 28, 1962, and NSC Executive Committee Record of Action, October 29, 1962, Meeting No. 12, *ibid*.

42. Agenda for Executive Committee Meeting, October 27, 1962, Box 49/Classified Subjects, Papers of Theodore Sorensen, JFK Library.

43. Walt Rostow to Edwin Martin, November 2, 1962: Memo on "The Non-Invasion Commitment," *ibid*; Hilsman, *The Move a Nation*, Chapter 14.

44. Donald C. Hafner, "Bureaucratic Politics and 'Those Frigging Missiles,' "

Orbis, Vol. 21 (Summer, 1977), pp. 307–333; See especially Paterson's "Fixation with Cuba" in his Kennedy's *Quest for Victory*, pp. 123–155.

45. "The Administration's Views on the Nuclear Test Ban Treaty," September 11, 1963, *Public Papers of the Presidents of the United States, John F. Kennedy, 1963* (Washington, D.C., 1964), pp. 669–671; Glenn T. Seaborg, *Kennedy, Khrushchev and the Test Ban* (Berkeley, 1981), p. 259.

46. NSC Memorandum on Cuba "Talking Points," March 4, 1963, Box 37A-38, NSF-Cuba, JFK Library.

CHAPTER 3

Visionary Diplomacy:
The Peace Corps and Food For Peace

It was the greatest adventure of the twentieth century, some believed. To others, like historian and Kennedy activist, James MacGregor Burns, this adventure encompassed the moral equivalent of Jefferson's commitment to democratic rights and Wilson's pursuit of international cooperation.[1] To Vice President Johnson's administrative assistant, Bill Moyers, the new agency was also "practical" and did "not promise the moon."[2] On the other hand, Dean Rusk and the State Department wondered if it remained too experimental.[3] General Bernard Hershey of the Selective Service worried it was an elaborate draft-dodging scheme, and R. Sargent Shriver, the president's politically enthusiastic brother-in-law, complained that this unusual new outfit might become a nursery for romantic incompetents.[4]

This controversial program was the Peace Corps. The president's own doubts about its usefulness contributed to the confusion. Food For Peace, a more specific international enterprise modeled off the Peace Corps approach, stimulated similar "official confusion" because of that very approach. Over a decade after Camelot, Arthur Schlesinger reflected on the Peace Corps, Food For Peace, and the "ask not what your country can do for you" spirit of volunteerism. Within days after Kennedy's death, volunteerism had already become an important component of the Kennedy legacy. Schlesinger considered the volunteerism development within the creation of a compassionate government. Yet, it also was a government run by tough-skinned cold warriors who never understood how committed their volunteers were to spreading American humanism abroad. Always railing against the "tired old men" of the Eisenhower White House, Kennedy in 1960 set the stage for a romantic view of diplomatic action. The stiff upper-lip, rules-bound Eisenhower embassies would soon be filled with young, pro-Kennedy reformists, working night and day to uplift the Third World masses and bring the largest measure of humanist concern to the anticommunist cause since the days of the Marshall Plan in post-World War II Europe. The Peace Corps would always symbolize this touch of romance, this belief in the power of citizen action. Food For Peace would maintain yet another dash of romance, but its operation would become quickly entangled with another Kennedy mystique, and a less genial one than dispatching teachers and agrarian experts abroad, counterinsurgency.

THE PEACE CORPS

Winning "the hearts and minds" of the Third World in the battle for communist versus anticommunist allegiance required more than romance. Kennedy knew that from the beginning days of discussion over Peace Corps possibilities.[5] Championing American goodness abroad became a welcome issue to the 1960 electorate, he discovered. The trick was to wed "goodness policies" to his more well-known "massive retaliation" hard line against communist expansion. He also had to convince himself that American goodness could indeed be expressed through a workable policy.[6] He remained unconvinced as late as November 1963. Despite the glowing rhetoric on behalf of citizen action overseas, there is little evidence to suggest that Kennedy found it truly necessary to cold war victory.

Not surprisingly, considering Kennedy's interest in the text, *The Ugly American* donated the Peace Corps idea through the activities of its hero, Homer Atkins. Portrayed as a retired construction engineer and self-made millionaire, Atkins volunteered his expertise in the fictional Southeast Asian country of Sarkhan. Once there, he discovered American aid programs ineffective. They were administered, he observed, by a bizarre crowd of empire builders. Atkins assaulted U.S. foreign aid experts for attempting to integrate big New Deal-styled projects into a nonreceptive culture, suggesting smaller projects that involve a certain people-to-people approach. He proved the point by inventing an irrigation process using local materials and involving the full support of the villagers. No policy was imposed upon them, and the cross-cultural contacts were invaluable to American anticommunist endeavors. A local mechanic even became his manufacturing partner, who, in turn, helped others abandon their view of a tyrannical, uncaring America.[7]

Although the Atkins tale stressed volunteerism, expertise, small worthy projects, and cross-cultural communication, it also suggested that American values of self-help and free enterprise could be applied anywhere if the locals were pushed hard enough to accept them. Cold war victory, therefore, became closer to reality through such tactics. This message was clear to the political community who studied Homer Atkins's methods via *The Ugly American*. More "good guys" like Atkins, with their unique combined characteristics of populist and pragmatist, were needed in the service of America abroad. Small was indeed better, and the Third World needed trained, dedicated American advisors willing to adapt the culture of their host nation and village.

Shortly before the 1960 campaign was under full swing, Representative Henry Reuss introduced his Point 4 for Youth Bill. Citing *The Ugly American* as the reference for his legislation, Reuss had created the forerunner to Kennedy's Peace Corps organization. Volunteers were not to be sent en masse to any one location, thus avoiding the appearance of special preference towards one area. A five-year term of service would be set for the volunteer, preventing the creation of foreign service-like bureaucracies with protective turf and interest. Reuss worked with what he believed constituted the best messages of the Atkins tale, and he submitted his legislation to the Kennedy campaign for whatever political use. He was convinced that the new program would represent America's finest hour in foreign affairs during the 1960s. Kennedy disagreed, noting that it could never be "central" to U.S. anticommunist policies.[8]

Kennedy's chief rival in the early primaries, Senator Hubert Humphrey of Minnesota, took up the Reuss cause, coined the term Peace Corps, and attempted to attack Kennedy on his lack of liberal innovation. It became part of a last-ditch Humphrey campaign effort that failed. In any event, Reuss and Humphrey had created the Peace Corps as an election issue.[9] Kennedy now had to assess its political worthiness and perhaps discard his doubts about its cold war practicality. The alternative was to permit his Republican opponent, Vice President Nixon, to steal the issue, champion its "new directions," and deaden the Kennedy attack against Eisenhower's "tired old men."

Whereas Kennedy wondered if a Peace Corps of enthusiastic college graduates could truly plant the seeds of American-styled democracies abroad, no one questioned the nature of the Peace Corps mission.[10] Was it an expression of Jeffersonian idealism, or was it a new version of imperial arrogance? A returning Peace Corps volunteer of the 1960s told the press that her job had been to "create little Americans" out of Thai villagers, and that the task had been foolish and self-destructive. Were smaller projects really more helpful to American anticommunist efforts in the Third World, especially if the U.S. helped maintain a repressive regime over these projects?[11] Even Kennedy's own early studies on the issue could not answer that question the way everyone wished to hear it. Meanwhile, the reaction of some political conservatives was unexpected. The Democrats had labeled the Peace Corps a liberal issue. Consequently, it held liabilities in a usually conservative America. The Peace Corps promise of smaller is better, on the other hand, also promised a lower foreign aid budget to countries whose pro-Americanism had been in doubt. Kennedy found plenty of conservative support on that point alone.[12]

Although he arrived after midnight, candidate Kennedy would find nearly 10,000 students on October 14, 1960, at the University of Michigan–Ann Arbor waiting for the announcement of a bold, new volunteers program. The Massachusetts senator did not disappoint them. Calling for a new spirit of selfless involvement, he asked the students to spend the coming decade in Asia or Africa. Through the great personal sacrifice of skilled young Americans, the downtrodden would be uplifted and the cold war would wither. The crowd went wild, and a tired Kennedy, who had manufactured the speech as he went along, was shocked at the reaction.[13]

He delivered two more polished versions of the Michigan speech before the end of the campaign. The most literate and memorable of the two was at San Francisco's Cow Palace on November 2, 1960. It pulled together the "tired old men" theme and the Atkins tale, with the Reuss-Humphrey Peace Corps plan. Suggesting that American embassies were run by men "without compassion" for their host country's citizenry, he called for a direct link between America's gifted and talented and the struggling and illiterate of the developing world.[14] A new age of the caring America was about to begin. Admitting that the life of the unpaid Peace Corps worker would not be easy, Kennedy still pre-

dicted great long-term benefits to American interests through these sac-
rifices.

> But if the life will not be easy, it will be rich and satisfying. For every
> young American who participates in the Peace Corps—who works in a
> foreign land—will know that he or she is sharing in the great common
> task of bringing to man that decent way of life which is the foundation
> of freedom and a condition of peace.[15]

With the press calling the Peace Corps "the best fresh idea of the
campaign," the Kennedy team believed it had "one up" on Nixon during the last days of the 1960 election.[16] It would take several months
for Kennedy to view the Peace Corps idea as more than just a political
football. Indeed, Nixon, shortly before election day, expressed the need
for "teams of agronomists and public nurses" abroad, but his words
lacked a certain focus. More to the point, Nixon would have preferred
to attack Kennedy's Peace Corps plan as a draft-dodging mechanism,
but the unexpected popularity of the plan forced him to echo it within
his own campaign.[17] It was too late.

The Peace Corps announcement was a good political tactic in 1960;
however, John and Robert Kennedy rated their grassroots campaign
style more essential to victory than any one foreign policy-related suggestion. Although they felt bound to make good on their word, there
was little enthusiasm for the Peace Corps mission. Bidding farewell to
young volunteers about to leave for two years of service in Asia or
Africa provided great photo opportunities for Kennedy's youthful image
as well as for the possibility of impassioned anticommunist rhetoric.
Hence, he told the cabinet in 1961 that the Peace Corps was "good
public relations and very American."[18] Both volunteers and Washing-
ton-based Peace Corps personnel detected sarcasm and cynicism in
Kennedy's voice during the president's address to the first group of
several hundred Peace Corps trainees. "Our Peace Corps," he said with
an enigmatic smile, "is not designed as an instrument of diplomacy or
propaganda or ideological conflict. It is designed to permit our people
to exercise more fully their responsibilities in the great common cause
of world development."[19]

Reminding many of a younger version of the always energetic Hubert
Humphrey, R. Sargent Shriver, the coordinator of the Chicago Board

of Education and the president's brother-in-law, was selected as Peace Corps director. Believing the rhetoric he heard, Shriver promised a tireless commitment to the success of Peace Corps. He assumed the new agency would stand on its own, unbound to the budgets or directives of existing government bodies. With characteristic vigor, optimism, and bright-eyed presentation, Shriver told the press in March 1961 that the Peace Corps would become the vanguard of cold war victory by 1970. It would even add a new dimension to American education within the tradition of learning by doing.[20]

Surrounded by educators and labor leaders and his division chiefs, Shriver also brought aboard cost analysis experts like Ralph Lazarus, president of the Federated Department Stores in Cincinnati, to assure that a worldwide budget would be used effectively. Moral projects and set budgets, Shriver told his staff, rarely mix well in American history. The resettlement work of FDR's War Refugee Board at the end of World War II or the Freedman's Bureau of the Civil War era were two examples of noble projects that ignored budgetary realities. The Peace Corps, he vowed, would never face these problems.[21]

To Shriver, the Kennedy administration enjoyed the opportunity to "take the world by surprise and prove that the American revolution is on the move again."[22] Although unknown to Shriver, the president regarded such ambitions as rather silly. Soon to discover this opinion by the end of 1961, the Peace Corps director continued to champion great goals for his organization and provided Kennedy with the requested visibility. He fought hard and won, thanks to his own public charisma and political determination, to keep the Peace Corps from becoming a forgettable division of the Agency for International Development (AID). Kennedy had assumed that would become the fate of the Peace Corps after the campaign-related euphoria wore away. Shriver made it clear to the president that the euphoria would remain throughout the first term. He threatened to resign if the Peace Corps was not given a chance, and he warned the White House that the electorate saw his agency as vital to U.S. foreign policy.[23] Shriver kept his job, Congress remained happy to fund him, and Kennedy continued to be surprised at the continued excitement in the nation over a minor facet of cold war confrontation.

Kennedy never understood the pro-Peace Corps public opinion, but the public thought he did. Even the press, at a joint Peace Corps–State Department briefing in 1961, applauded the enthusiasm of the following

Shriver assessment, and linked it, of course, to Kennedy's own perceived sentiments about the agency.

> When our young people go to live and work in foreign countries, in villages and schools in the developing nations of the world, when they put their hands and their skills to work in the development of this two-thirds of the world which is struggling to advance out of poverty, they are going to make a real contribution, I believe, to world peace. For economic growth in these nations is one of the conditions of peace, and better understanding among people is one of the conditions of peace. And the Peace Corps, we hope, will contribute to both.[24]

Although they spent varying periods of several weeks in intensive language, cultural, and political training, the first five thousand Peace Corps volunteers of the Kennedy era reached their rural Third World assignments ill-prepared. Crash courses in language and cultural mores rarely rescued middle-class American youth from the reality of Asian and African poverty. Kennedy found the liberal political profile of the Peace Corps volunteer embarrassing to the generally conservative cause of die-hard anticommunism, and the press discovery of several far-leftist applicants to the Peace Corps added further embarrassments. Indeed, the 1961 volunteers group to Latin America sent Kennedy a petition, gathered at a meeting in Bogota, which asked the question why they should spend "their youthful days in the boondocks at $75 per month" when the president spends as much "for lunch." He was also asked to set a less elitist example of American life to the Third World. Shriver thought Kennedy would find the petition amusing, and he did.[25]

Shriver was also not averse to perking Kennedy's interest in the Peace Corps through unconventional means. He provided, for instance, photographs and biographies of what were called "cover girl" volunteers for the president's enjoyment. The "cover girl" files always focused on an attractive, usually well-endowed female volunteer in her early twenties, with the recommendation that she visit the White House following her term of service. Shriver usually noted wryly that the girls were valuable to "foreign affairs," but "probably couldn't type."[26] Kennedy thanked Shriver for the files, but the terms of service for the girls expired after his assassination.

Since Kennedy believed that the cold war in the Third World would be won or lost first in the Asian/Pacific region, the Peace Corps volunteers to leading nonaligned nations, such as Ahmed Sukarno's Indonesia, were considered part of an important "hearts and minds" policy. Yet, direct diplomacy, threats of war, and war itself elsewhere in Southeast Asia would determine the full nature of U.S. relations in that region.[27] The Peace Corps had its greatest impact where Kennedy thought it would be truly a "lost adventure," Africa. The locations were too remote and the cultures too primitive, he believed, for the Peace Corps to make a difference.[28] He was wrong.

In Sierra Leone, for example, the political leadership agreed that "the Peace Corps has shown us a world we never knew existed. Some of us had never seen a truck or lorry or people from the outside who wanted to help us. We had heard of America, but now we know what it means."[29] During and after the Cuban missile crisis when Premier Khrushchev began a desperate campaign to convince African Third World leaders that America despised the struggling people of Cuba, threatened them with nuclear oblivion, and would do the same, if given the chance, to Africans, most African nations rejected this type of appeal. A number of West African politicians cited the Peace Corps as the basis for their rejection, because Americans appeared willing to help Africans and not destroy them. That fact, combined with improving race relations in the United States, and better respect in Washington for black African diplomats assigned there, guaranteed failure for Khrushchev.[30] Kennedy found the Peace Corps impact amazing, but it did not enliven his attitude toward the agency. Their efforts in Africa, he concluded, were part of larger policies.[31] Meanwhile, the future of U.S.-African relations appeared uncertain.

By 1963, some of Kennedy's closest aides, such as McGeorge Bundy, were breaking away from the president's "don't give a damn" approach to the Peace Corps. Bundy declared it "growing in value" in January 1963, and asked Shriver to get more involved in international hot spots, such as Algeria. Free from French rule for only a matter of months, Algeria had been a sore point in U.S.-French relations. Kennedy had seen the French-Algerian war of 1954–1962 as a classic colonial conflict and not a French assault on Algerian communism. A Peace Corps mission there would demonstrate U.S. support for recently decolonized nations, even though the action might disturb a long-time but contentious ally, France. Bundy believed that Shriver's "help here might butter a lot of parsnips," i.e., elevate America's pro-Third World image within the Third World. More to the point, Bundy said he would back Shriver in any Algerian debate with his brother-in-law.[32] The Peace Corps director was flattered by the new attentions from the White House, but he never saw his agency as a political football. Unless a real commitment existed to use the Peace Corps in its usual humanitarian fashion, Shriver saw no place for it in Algeria and no place for it in the middle of a possible U.S. versus France row.[33] He won his case.

By late 1963, the original group of volunteers were about to complete their terms of service and were due back in Washington by January 1964. These volunteers could credit themselves for having founded the modern secondary school system of Ghana and having constituted 90 percent of all degree-holding teachers in Liberia and one-third of all secondary school instructors in Ethiopia.[34] The Marxist rebels who seized power in Ethiopia during the 1970s would later claim, and often not in jest, that they learned everything they knew about revolutionary action from Kennedy-era Peace Corps volunteers.

In Latin America, the accomplishments stressed basic infrastructure improvements. For example, in Colombia, Peace Corps volunteers supervised the building of thirty aqueducts, forty-nine roads, and fourteen bridges. In Chile, two hundred schools were constructed. At the same time, Peace Corps volunteers in Asia were granted the Ramon Magsaysay Award, Asia' s equivalent to the Nobel Peace Prize, for their work in eleven Asian nations. The award noted that "in twenty-two months of quiet labor, Peace Corps volunteers who came to this part of the world have secured a verdict not before vouchsafed to any other foreign group. Peace Corps workers achieved in less than two years an understanding with Asian peoples that promises to pass all tests."[35]

Shriver was able to deliver these glowing tributes to Congress in his requests for more funding in the coming 1964 election year. He admitted to a closed session of the House Foreign Affairs Committee that many well-qualified, recent applicants had been turned away because they saw the job in too romantic a light. Others, already in service, he said, sometimes tried to save the world on their own terms. Hence, he regretted their dispatching overseas. A higher stipend and congressional guarantees of a job for a returning volunteer might increase applications and help better weed out problem cases. The Congress, he learned, had little interest in playing personnel director for the Peace Corps.

Yet, something had to be done. Host countries demanded more volunteers, particularly in the science and medical fields. Shriver requested $108 million for 1964 in order to support a goal of 13,000 volunteers. He won close to $102 million to support 11,300 volunteers, and was asked to return funds if the goal was not reached. Only half the goal was attained, for few applicants met the rigid language, intellectual, and physical requirements of an always demanding training schedule. A certain Kennedy model of the perfect New Frontiersman applied to the volunteer: brilliant, dedicated, physically powerful, with a touch of ruthlessness. Nevertheless, the program continued to attract more visionaries than supermen.[36] Shriver saw the matter as a problem in supply and demand, since he could not always meet the requests of Third World nations for volunteers. Kennedy, despite his own reputation, simply had limited respect for visionaries representing American foreign policy. They continued to cloud U.S. initiatives with their own interpretations. He gave no examples.[37]

Harris Wofford, a U.S. senator from Pennsylvania, who was a Peace Corps director in Ethiopia for Kennedy as well as a Kennedy civil rights advisor and good friend, said in 1970 that his late boss saw the Peace Corps as a "peculiar but relatively benevolent combination of propaganda and charity, somewhat galling but to be accepted and put to use."[38] In 1966, Frank Mankiewicz, long-time Democratic party activist and Kennedy confidant noted that the president never doubted the Peace Corps, and that by late 1963 he saw the agency as an agent of great social change abroad. Kennedy's thinking on all cold war issues, Mankiewicz recalled, had begun to change following the assassination of South Vietnam's Diem in early November 1963.[39] Analyst David Riesman explained in 1966 that Kennedy, had he lived, would have cultivated the knowledge of returning Peace Corps volunteers to create a workable Third World policy in his second term.[40] Dean Rusk said that Kennedy "never" mentioned the Corps to him, for it "never" could be a part of America's foreign policy process. Its role was to "contribute" to foreign policy.[41] Finally, the *New Republic* and even a study by Radcliffe College, which contributed more than one thousand volunteers in the early 1960s, explained that Kennedy "had always wanted to integrate returning volunteers into the federal government bureaucracy" because their New Frontier zeal would change bureaucracy forever and for the better.[42]

With the exception of Wofford's observations, the conclusions of the Kennedy watchers above remain most speculative. Even Rusk's implication that Kennedy "never" thought about the Corps at all stretches the truth. While Shriver saw the Peace Corps as a useful tool abroad and Kennedy grabbed whatever political mileage it would give him, they both considered the agency innovative, experimental, and capable of doing some good somewhere. It was a simple assessment in a complex time. Many Kennedy observers believed that the bright, eloquent young Harvard-graduate president had to be complex in all matters of decision making. That was not the case here and they had difficulty accepting it.

FOOD FOR PEACE

To Kennedy, humanism and realism came together effectively to benefit cold war victory when the policy, or agency, provided immediate, practical results within the anticommunist cause. Food For Peace did a better job in that regard. Kennedy consistently compared it to the Peace Corps, and, although its mandate held higher cold war esteem to the president than the Peace Corps, its humanist edge still made it of limited value to the White House in the larger scheme of things.

It was Dean Rusk, the self-proclaimed crusty Georgian and gentleman farmer, who suggested to Kennedy in January 1961 that under proper auspices and a decent director, America could brandish its agricultural surplus abroad as a Third World lure away from procommunist attractions.[43] Combining humanism and anticommunist goals remained in the cold war traditions of the Marshall Plan and were consistent, in basic form, with the Peace Corps approach.

Food For Peace was nothing new. When Kennedy entered the White House, Food For Peace already operated under the legislative umbrella of the Agricultural Trade Development and Assistance Act of 1954 (Public Law 480). Almost immediately after it was established, it became a forgotten, low-priority office with a budget to match. Trapped in the days of the "bigger bang for the buck" diplomacy of Eisenhower and Secretary of State Dulles, Food For Peace, between July 1954 and January 1961, had exported a meager twelve million tons of surplus food and fiber. Following Kennedy's action on Rusk's recommendation, the program exported thirty-three million tons in 1961 alone, even offering long-term food supply guarantees to India and Pakistan. This action was in addition to administering emergency feeding programs in disaster-stricken countries. By late 1961, Food For Peace fed ten million grade schoolers through lunch programs overseas, fed political refugees, and established food development programs in eleven countries.[44]

The arranging of contracts for these projects involved greater efforts than the dispatching of Peace Corps volunteers. A school lunch program in Laos, for instance, required the coordination of interests within the host government and America's Department of Agriculture, AID, and the State Department. The contractors would meet in Washington, on occasion, to assure that all of their concerns were being addressed in individual programs. When he was not on-site overseas with a program, the Food For Peace director was expected to play referee in Washington with the competing contracting partners. Kennedy liked the approach. It reflected his admiration for the squabbling cabinet figures of the FDR era and the "may the best policy survive" attitude that governed their New Deal decisions. The Food For Peace director saw that approach as confusing, and he soon learned it would permit the president to take advantage of the situation for the benefit of other policies.[45]

George McGovern was that beleaguered Food For Peace director. A World War II Army Air Corps hero turned struggling politician, McGovern enjoyed the reputation in his native South Dakota of a vigorous young Democrat who "triumphed in the face of adversity." As the only Democratic party member of Congress in his home state during the 1950s, McGovern single-handedly rebuilt the Democratic party there. Democratic party lore, as early as 1961, told of the days when the South Dakota headquarters of the party once consisted of McGovern's station wagon. A history professor, and admirer of Woodrow Wilson as well as of Democrat-turned-Progressive Henry Wallace, McGovern favored less rather than more militancy in cold war policies.[46]

The undersecretary of state, George Ball, recommended McGovern for the job on the basis of a little-known May 1959 speech he had made on behalf of halting the appeal of communism through a new international food policy.

"Give us this day our daily bread," is still the prayer of human beings in the far corners of the earth. . . . I become more convinced each day that our most powerful material asset in building a world of peace and freedom is our food abundance. The hungry multitudes of Asia, Africa, and the Middle East are far more interested in bread, medical care and schools than in any number of jets and Sputniks. Does anyone wonder what the crafty Khrushchev would do if he had America's surplus food to use in his international operations?[47]

Kennedy paraphrased the McGovern speech in January 1961 when he announced the new, more ambitious version of Food For Peace and the South Dakotan as its head. McGovern made it clear to Kennedy from the beginning that the program, as designed, would not stop a communist revolution. Instead, it would have a long-term impact on positive Third World attitudes toward America. That was consistent, he believed, with Kennedy's "take the first step" theme to cold war victory. Kennedy, on the other hand, preferred more immediate accomplishments, regardless of campaign themes. Those efforts would be consistent with eroding the image of the "Ugly American" in the Third World, a priority task for the president.[48]

The debate between Kennedy and McGovern over the mission of Food For Peace revolved around one basic point. McGovern saw the program as an effort to help the common citizens of Third World nations. Kennedy saw it as an effort to maintain governments friendly to the American view. Particularly in Southeast Asia, McGovern's largest problem involved the corruption of pro-U.S. officials who stole excess Food For Peace deliveries to benefit their own political and financial position. McGovern complained to Washington; however, he also learned of a Kennedy decision, as early as March 1961, to employ "flexible tools" when dealing with Food For Peace objectives. "Flexible tools" was Kennedy's jargon for Central Intelligence Agency (CIA) penetration of daily Food For Peace operations in Southeast Asia. In short, the CIA assured key government leaders, namely in South Vietnam and Laos, that food stocks would always be available for their personal needs in exchange for the more ruthless prosecution of the communist insurgencies plaguing their governments.[49]

McGovern saw the "flexible tools" approach, about which he learned by accident, as a betrayal of his trust and that of hungry people throughout the Third World. Kennedy, on the other hand, viewed Food For Peace as part of a larger counterinsurgency effort and not in McGovern's raw humanitarian terms. The Truman Doctrine, under which American anticommunism still operated, favored the destruction of communist expansion. It said nothing about uplifting democratic idealism in Third World nations or feeding the starving masses. These were hard-nosed realities for America to face because of the doctrine. Indeed, the "Ugly American" had resulted from this approach.

With Food For Peace, Kennedy could enjoy the best of both anticommunist worlds. He could prop up existing pro-Western regimes, corrupt or not, and he could demonstrate American decency at the same time. The trick was to avoid too strong a connection to corruption, or the humanism of Food For Peace would be undermined by "Ugly American" charges. It was a delicate game, and McGovern preferred to return to the tough politics of South Dakota than participate with Kennedy's "flexible tools." The episode would sour McGovern on anticommunist causes of most any design, making him an early doubter of Washington's Vietnam War decisions and a later champion of U.S. military withdrawal from Southeast Asia.

Kennedy was an expert at providing visions of America to a receptive audience and then declaring them fact. The vision of the invaluable Peace Corps representing America's best self abroad, and Food For Peace, the vision of a food-rich nation indiscriminately donating its wealth to the world's hungry, were Kennedy-established images that grew in stature after his death. The tales of CIA intrigue vis-à-vis Food For Peace, or Kennedy's cynical rejection of the Peace Corps mission, began to emerge during the soul-searching days of the post-Vietnam era. The old yellow press dictum of "when the legend is bigger than truth, print the legend" has applied well to the public memory of Kennedy in this regard. The Peace Corps remains the symbol of Kennedy's "ask not. . . . " volunteerism, and recent public opinion credits Kennedy's commitment to the task, while Food For Peace remains a lesser known story.

To Kennedy, both the Peace Corps and Food For Peace were adventures in counterinsurgency. Peace Corps volunteers sabotaged procommunist sentiment at the village level and CIA operatives assigned to Food For Peace appealed to Third World corruption in the name of national self-interest. A generation after Camelot, volunteerism as a means to achieve cold war victory appears naive, even to former New Frontiersmen. Indeed, the Kennedy commitment to cold war victory now appears both naive and deadly to the same individuals.

Sargent Shriver finds the Peace Corps volunteer of the 1990s more skillful, more intelligent, more mature, and more realistic than the original volunteer group. Today's volunteer is often a retired technologist rather then a freshly graduated liberal arts major. Most volunteer to help others overseas as opposed to the New Frontier-era motivation of helping America kill the appeal of communism. Shriver admits that he admires the practicality of the 1990s Peace Corps, but that a dash of romance is not necessarily a bad thing. The problem with the Peace Corps of the early 1960s, Shriver stresses, was that the program was new and untried, the president was obsessed with cold war priorities, and the Kennedy team believed they were invincible.[50]

American invincibility in the cold war, associated with the "can do" philosophy of the Kennedy family, dominated the volunteerism decisions. The president was politically astute enough to keep his reservations about the Peace Corps/Food For Peace policies to himself, for the public did not need to know that their faith in these policies was misplaced. Moreover, Kennedy especially learned during the missile crisis that the electorate favored peace to "massive retaliation." It helped to explain the public's warm approval of the serene Peace Corps/Food For Peace approach to foreign policy. It did not mean that Kennedy had to accept the explanation. He had created the new era of volunteerism, and he took his doubts about that accomplishment with him to Dallas.

ENDNOTES

1. Thomas Cronin, "On the American Presidency: A Conversation with James MacGregor Burns," *Presidential Studies Quarterly*, Vol. XVI, No. 3, Summer 1986, pp. 533–534.
2. Moyers to Sargent Shriver, February 27, 1961, Box 3/Organizational Folder #2, The Peace Corps Papers of Gerald W. Bush, JFK Library.
3. Shriver to Kennedy, January 1, 1961, Box 85, POF/Peace Corps, JFK Library.
4. *Ibid.*
5. Shriver to Chester Bowles, undersecretary of state for political affairs, February 23, 1961, Box 3/Organizational Folder #2, Bush Papers, JFK Library.
6. Kennedy to Salinger, March 1, 1961, Box 3/History of the Peace Corps, Bush Papers, JFK Library.
7. See the opening chapters to Lederer and Burdick's *Ugly American*.
8. Henry Reuss, "A Foreign Aid Program That Went Astray," 1960 Position Paper available in Box 3/History of the Peace Corps, Bush Papers, JFK Library, or in the Reuss Records of the 5th District-Milwaukee, Marquette University, Milwaukee, Wisconsin; Kennedy to Rusk, March 1, 1961, Box 3/History of the Peace Corps, Bush Papers, JFK Library.
9. Sargent Shriver, *Point of the Lance* (New York, 1964), pp. 1–13.
10. Peace Corps Memo: "Legislative Issues and Preparation," March 2, 1961, Box 3/Organizational Folder #2, JFK Library.
11. Critical accounts of the Peace Corps record based on disillusioned and concerned Peace Corps volunteers' reports is the basis of Gerald T. Rice, *The Bold Experiment* (South Bend, IN, 1985), pp. 1–66.
12. Sargent Shriver, "The Best Job in Washington," (manuscript submitted to *New York Times*, May 2, 1963), Boc 86, POF, JFK Library.

13. Ann Arbor Speech (October 14, 1960), and JFK to RFK, October 15, 1960 Campaign Files/Michigan correspondence, JFK Library.
14. Gary May, "Passing the Torch and Lighting Fires," *Kennedy's Quest for Victory*, p. 285.
15. Kennedy repeated these comments for his major presidential address on the Peace Corps in early 1961. Statement by President Kennedy, March 1, 1961, Box 3/History, Bush Papers, JFK Library.
16. See the opening chapter to Gerald T. Rice, *Twenty Years of Peace Corps* (Washington, D.C., 1981).
17. State Department Memo: "Establishment of the Peace Corps," March 1, 1961, Box 3/History, Bush Papers, JFK Library.
18. State Department Memo: "Peace Corps Role in U.S. Foreign Policy," March 25, 1963, Box 284/Peace Corps, NSF, JFK Library.
19. Gerald W. Bush, "President Kennedy's New AID," Classified booklet for senior AID administrators, pp. 17–19, March 1961, and Kennedy Statement, March 1, 1961, Box 1/AID and Box 3/History, Bush Papers, JFK Library.
20. Harris Wofford, *Of Kennedys and Kings* (New York, 1980), pp. 253–262; "Transcript of Background Press and Radio News Briefing with Mr. Shriver," March 6, 1961, Box 1/Basic Design, Bush Papers, JFK Library.
21. *Ibid.*; and Edward R. Murrow, AID director, to Shriver, March 14, 1961, Box 3/Organization, Bush Papers, JFK Library.
22. Shriver to Ed Beyley, administrative assistant to Governor Gaylord Nelson (D. Wisc.), March 6, 1961, Box 1/Basic Design, Bush Papers, JFK Library.
23. Shriver to Kennedy, January 1961; Shriver to Kennedy, July 1961; "Joint State-USIA-Peace Corps Message," August 15, 1961, Box 85, POF/Peace Corps, and Box 3/Organization, Bush Papers, JFK Library.
24. *Ibid.*; Shriver Press Briefing, March 6, 1961, Box 1/Basic Design, Bush Papers, JFK Library.
25. Shriver to Kennedy, December 1961 (Report on Peace Corps Activities, July 1961–December 1961); Shriver testimony to House Committee on Foreign Affairs, October 15, 1963; Shriver to Kennedy, n.d. (probably December 1961), Box 85/Peace Corps, POF and Box 1/Congressional Presentation, Bush Papers, JFK Library.
26. Shriver to Kennedy, n.d. (probably June 1963), Box 86/Peace Corps, POF, JFK Library.
27. Timothy P. Maga, "The New Frontier vs. Guided Democracy: JFK, Sukarno and Indonesia, 1961–1963," *Presidential Studies Quarterly*, Vol. XX, No. 1, Winter 1990, pp. 91–102.
28. Shriver testimony to House Committee on Foreign Affairs, October 15, 1963; Harris Wofford, "The Future of the Peace Corps," *Annals of the American Academy of Political and Social Science* (1970); Frank Mankiewicz, "The Peace Corps: A Revolutionary Force, Peace Corps Discussion Paper, 1966," Box 1/Congressional Presentation and Box 3/Future of Peace Corps, Bush Papers, JFK Library.

29. Shriver to Kennedy (Volunteers Reports), May 2, 1963, Box 86, POF/Peace Corps, JFK Library.
30. *Ibid*. See also Chapter 6 of this book.
31. Rusk to U.S. embassies in Peace Corps-hosted nations, Classified Report: "Peace Corps Role in U.S. Foreign Policy, March 25, 1963," Box 284, NSF/Peace Corps, JFK Library.
32. Bundy to Shriver, January 19, 1963, *ibid*.
33. Shriver to Bundy, *ibid*.
34. Shriver testimony to the House Committee on Foreign Affairs, October 15, 1963, Box 1/Congressional Presentation, Bush Papers, JFK Library.
35. *Ibid*.
36. *Ibid*.; Wofford, "Future of the Peace Corps," Box 3/Future of the Peace Corps, Bush Papers, JFK Library.
37. Confidential Memo: "The Peace Corps Since Kennedy," Shriver to Peace Corps directorship, April 1965, Box 1/Authority and Legislative History, Bush Papers, JFK Library.
38. Wofford, "Future of the Peace Corps," Box 3/Future of the Peace Corps, Bush Papers, JFK Library.
39. Frank Mankiewicz, "The Peace Corps: A Revolutionary Force," Peace Corps Discussion Paper: 1966, *ibid*.
40. David Riesman, "Terrifying and Illuminating," Peace Corps Discussion Papers, 1966, *ibid*.
41. Rusk to U.S. Embassies in Peace Corps-hosted nations, March 25, 1963, Box 284, NSF/Peace Corps, JFK Library; Shriver, *Point of the Lance*, p. 72.
42. "Peace Corps' Daring New Look," *The New Republic*, February 5, 1966, p. 19 Box 3/Future of the Peace Corps, Bush Papers, JFK Library.
43. Rusk to Kennedy, January 27, 1961, Box 87/Department of State, POF, JFK Library.
44. Official History: "The Food For Peace Program, Mission and Operation," March 1962, WH-9/Food For Peace, Schlesinger papers, JFK Library.
45. George McGovern, Food For Peace director, to Kennedy, March 10, 1961 and report: "Food For Peace: Appraisal and Recommendation," Box 78/Food For Peace Program, POF, JFK Library.
46. Rusk to Kennedy, January 27, 1961, and Gerald W. Bush, *President Kennedy's New AID* (AID publication, March 1961), Box 87/Department of State, POF, JFK Library and Box 1/AID Message, Bush Papers, JFK Library.
47. Official History, March 1962, WH-9/Food For Peace, Schlesinger Papers, JFK Library.
48. Kennedy to Congress, "Special Message on Foreign Aid and Food For Peace," March 22, 1961, Box 1/AID Message, Bush Papers, JFK Library.
49. McGovern to Kennedy, March 10, 1961, *ibid*.
50. Thomas Moore & Marianna Knight "Idealism's Rebirth," *U.S. News and World Report*, October 24, 1988, pp. 37–40.

CHAPTER 4

Great Adventure or Quagmire? Vietnam and the New Pacific Community

To those leaders who suffer an early death, history provides the legacy of promise. Stirring rhetoric characterizes them. In hindsight, the observer can conclude that they were destined to greatness. It remains their good luck to be assessed less by their accomplishments than by their inspiration. Without a doubt, all of us would welcome such pleasant judgment of ourselves. Kennedy's assassination spared him from difficult decisions concerning Vietnam. Few remember him as a "Vietnam president." Nevertheless, his public affirmations of the inaugural vow to "bear any burden" in the cold war suggest that military escalation would have continued had he lived. His private meetings about the matter suggest confusion, stimulated not by concern over the possibility of horrible war but by frustration over the elusive cold war victory.

As always, decisions over the nature of American's role in Vietnam were made in the luxury of worldwide military supremacy and a recent record of military invincibility. As always, Kennedy provided the additional luxury of academic-styled debate over Vietnam policy options and considerations.[1] Hence, historians like Arthur Schlesinger have claimed, via assessments of one option versus another, that American military withdrawal would have been inevitable during a Kennedy second term.[2] Yet, at the same time, historians like Thomas Paterson have claimed that large-scale escalation might have come sooner than even President Johnson's decision.[3] The "what might have happened" question looms large for those who hoped for a different conclusion to America's 1975 defeat in Vietnam. That Kennedy would have offered a solution, either military withdrawal or military victory, remains an intriguing prospect to many. Unless Kennedy privately harbinged a secret plan and took it with him to Dallas in November 1963, the evidence only offers the usual twists and turns of the Kennedy decision-making process.

Kennedy optimism over cold war victory in Vietnam was best manifested in the elaborate 1961 plan for a new international organization of Asian/Pacific states. Called the New Pacific Community, this organization, led behind the scenes by the United States, would eventually supercede U.N. and Southeast Asia Treaty Organization (SEATO) operations in the Asian/Pacific region with anticommunist military and economic programs largely financed by the Kennedy administration. Through "international cooperation," the violence of the Vietnam situation would be isolated and contained by the mid-1960s and cold war victory declared over the entire Asian/Pacific theatre by 1970.[4] Designed in secret between February and November 1961, the New Pacific Community remained the Kennedy team's best, yet most dreamlike plan for a pax Americana throughout the Asian/Pacific world. Although it met plenty of denunciations overseas as a vehicle for self-serving American policy, the plan was still on Kennedy's mind in November 1963.[5]

As a World War II-Pacific war hero who owed his life to Pacific islanders, as well as a former member of the Senate Subcommittee for Asian/Pacific Affairs, Kennedy would claim personal interests, along with some expertise, in the Asian/Pacific region. In fact, he made those claims loud and clear in speeches from Los Angeles to Seattle to Honolulu. Announcing that the world at half-century had now embarked in the "Pacific century," Senator Kennedy had once said the entire cold war would be won or lost in the Pacific. Praising the melting pot of Asian cultures in a variety of Asian/Pacific cities, he also noted that American cities could learn much about racial tolerance from the Asian/Pacific example.[6]

VIETNAM

Having toured the French bastion of Dien Bien Phu before its 1954 fall to Ho Chi Minh's National Liberation Front, Kennedy could even

claim on-site Vietnam experience. Following this tour, Senator Kennedy
had denounced French colonialism, providing later credibility to his
railings against the imperial qualities of "Ugly American" policies.
These attacks in the waning days of French rule in Vietnam largely
stressed France's military incompetence. Kennedy could, therefore, assault imperialism in later speeches, but also, with confidence, suggest
that America must always be more vigilant and competent than France
during any military contest with Asian communist rebels. He would
never view American policy as replacing French colonialism in Vietnam
or elsewhere in the region, for anticommunism need not take on colonial
aspects, he once noted, especially if America hoped to extinguish "Ugly
Americanism."[7]

As a member of the American Friends of Vietnam lobby group in
the 1950s, Kennedy had attacked the Eisenhower administration for not
making Vietnam a top policy priority. Consisting mostly of American
corporate investors in Vietnam and their conservative supporters in Congress, the American Friends of Vietnam encouraged the industries of
Massachusetts, which were growing at a faster rate than in other north-
eastern states, to share their economic success story with the newly
founded nation of South Vietnam.[8]

Kennedy had little personal interest in the language and ambitions
of private investment, despite his family's comfortable position vis-à-vis
successful business in Massachusetts. Championing business causes was
better suited for the Kennedys' Republican archrival Massachusetts
family, the Lodges.[9] Nevertheless, his speeches for the American Friends
of Vietnam painted an eloquent picture of a struggling but secure South
Vietnam that could be made more secure by an extremely attentive
Eisenhower administration and activist American business community.

> The independence of Free Vietnam is crucial to the free world in fields
> other than the military. Her economy is essential to the economy of all
> of Southeast Asia; and her political liberty is an inspiration to those
> seeking to obtain or maintain their liberty in all parts of Asia and indeed
> the world. The fundamental tenets of this nation's foreign policy, in short,
> depend in considerable measure upon a strong and free Vietnamese na-
> tion.[10]

Like any challenges to the established political order, Senator Kennedy reserved the right to assault the status quo but not, necessarily,
offer a workable alternative to it. During the late 1950s, he resurrected

his early 1950s speeches against French imperialism, noted how the Eishenhower White House had been too generous to the "colonial crowd" in Paris, and denounced American policy to Vietnam as too much propaganda and not enough aid. Complaining that nuclear superiority and military allowances were also not enough, he explained that teaching capitalism to impoverished Vietnamese might even be futile, and he worried that corruption in the South Vietnamese regime of Premier Ngo Dinh Diem might lure many to communism. His answer to these concerns was the same in every speech and to any audience.

> I shall not attempt to set forth the details of the type of aid program this nation should offer the Vietnamese—for it is not the details of that program that are as important as the spirit with which it is offered and the objectives it seeks to accomplish.[11]

The only other senator who made regular speeches for the American Friends of Vietnam was Mike Mansfield (D-Montana). Mansfield provided correspondence from Diem to fellow senators, urging his colleagues to support the premier's aid request. As a Catholic with middle-class roots and conservative politics in a country filled with Buddhist peasants and post-French Vietnam revolutionary fervor, Diem remained an embattled leader. Insisting on more U.S. aid, Diem believed his country deserved the high priority that Europe enjoyed in the heyday of the Marshall Plan. Mansfield worried that race, memories of the bitter and costly 1946–1954 Vietnamese-French War, and simple ignorance of Vietnamese affairs kept the American government from creating an intelligent response to Diem's appeal. To Mansfield, later a tireless critic of American military power in Vietnam, another expensive aid plan was in order. To Kennedy, any aid plan had to include the rebuilding of the Vietnamese military under U.S. guidance, technical advice on infrastructure matters, and even direct U.S. rule, if necessary, to rescue Vietnam from communist attractions.[12]

Free elections, as guaranteed by the 1954 Geneva Agreement, would make matters worse, Senator Kennedy claimed. Any election would be "stacked and subverted in advance," he said. They were to be avoided. The Eisenhower administration made the same point.[13] Yet, Kennedy's attacks on French colonialism and the latter's sad impact on poverty and illiteracy gave him the air of the concerned humanist. Combined with vague promises of direct U.S. control over Vietnamese economic projects and military affairs, Kennedy's campaign-related Vietnam policy constituted a "revolution" in American aid planning, or so the young senator declared. Although few in the U.S. electorate really cared, this approach to Vietnam distinguished Kennedy from other Democrats, such as Mansfield, as well as from the Eisenhower administration.[13]

These distinguishing marks did not necessarily promise improvements to policy making. Rather, they simply implied that America was "losing" the cold war in Southeast Asia, that a quick fix was elusive if not impossible, and Eisenhower was as much to blame as expanding communism. Labeling cold war policy as faltering remained a dangerous political gamble. Although Senator Joseph McCarthy had died in 1957, and his career had faded following Senate censuring of his Red baiting tactics three years earlier, the Wisconsin senator's brand of radical anti-communism still enjoyed many adherents at the time of the 1960 campaign.[14] Calling for a "revolution" in aid to South Vietnam, whether associated with the usual anti-"Ugly American" thesis or not, could easily backfire. Kennedy's "revolution" comments appeared too vague except in one area. American influence in South Vietnam, he stressed, was weak. By preaching failure in Vietnam, Kennedy, as a Vietnam policy-maker himself, could be accused by the electorate of providing that very failure. Noting that all was well in South Vietnam, and could be even better, would have been the safer tactic. Championing the campaign of brave new ideas that would "get America going again" at home and win the cold war abroad required bold rhetoric. Kennedy gambled with that rhetoric and won. The question remained if he believed his own rhetoric vis-à-vis "revolutionary" policies for South Vietnam, and if he intended to introduce these policies as president.

Was South Vietnam's future all that important to American security? The Vietnamese "would always be minor players in Pacific defense" according to Edmund Gullion, the chief of Eisenhower's Policy Planning Staff–Vietnam and a friend of Senator Kennedy. During a closed Senate hearing in the mid-1950s, Gullion, the former counselor of the U.S. Embassy–Saigon, told his friend and other senators that Vietnam was expendable to U.S. interests. Since nothing was expendable in the march to cold war victory, Kennedy would simply twist Gullion's comments to match his own campaign theme. He would then question Eisenhower's treatment of Vietnam as a "minor issue," yet never really explain how it was to become a "major issue."[15]

Associated with Kennedy's "major issue" theme was the assumption that failure to counter the aggression of Ho Chi Minh's North Vietnam, or that of the insurgents within South Vietnam, would be acquainted with appeasement. To Kennedy's generation, appeasement always meant the European democracies' accommodating policy towards Adolf Hitler's 1938 demands for the Sudetenland of Czechoslavakia. That accommodation, made in Munich, had become symbolic of foolish, self-destructive behavior on the part of democratic foreign policy. Any cry of "Munich" against the Kennedy administration could result in the political kiss of death for a cold warrior. Quoting Kennedy's 1961 position on Vietnam during a 1965 press conference, Lyndon Johnson remembered that the late president made frequent reference to Munich in Vietnam policy making. He specifically recalled him saying: "We learned from Hitler at Munich that success feeds the appetite of aggression. The battle would be renewed in one country and then another."[16] There could be no turning back from U.S. military intervention in Vietnam lest the memory of impotent democracy, i.e. Munich, be raised once again. That unfortunate label would be the ultimate irony for the entire "can do" Kennedy administration.[17] It had to be avoided at all cost.

Both political parties shared Kennedy's "Munich" fears. Only five years before Kennedy won the presidency, American politicians were overreacting to memories of Munich in a manner that would seem ridiculous to a later generation. For instance, following Eisenhower's return from a summit in Geneva, the president was expected to make a homecoming speech at an airport runway. Since it was raining when Eisenhower arrived, his staff awaited him with umbrellas in hand. Vice President Nixon remembered that Britain's former prime minister, Neville Chamberlain, had returned from the Munich conference to a rainy London and a speech which proclaimed "peace in our time." To some, Chamberlain's very umbrella had become a symbol of appeasement. Nixon ordered the president's staff to keep their umbrellas at the office in order to avoid any Munich comparisons. Eisenhower gave his speech in the pouring rain.[18] These moist precautions did not stop Senator Kennedy from commenting that he "worried" about Eisenhower's gentlemanlike diplomacy with communist diplomats.[19] He did not explain his comments, but the implication was clear to his audience. The Eisenhower administration failed to champion U.S. interests in a strong enough fashion with the Soviets. In the cold war, this weakness was the hated equivalent of Munich-styled appeasement.

How real was this alleged U.S. government attraction to appeasement? Was there an element of truth to it all? Even an accusor like Kennedy would have answered these questions with difficulty. The need to avoid an "Asian Munich" was a familiar line uttered by Dean Rusk in Kennedy cabinet meetings on Vietnam.[20] Without question, Kennedy welcomed the suggestion that America must avoid any arrangement that grants a political advantage to Vietnamese communists. Yet, at the same time, he could explain to an old friend that the fear of another Munich was exaggerated and that his own career had helped along these exaggerations. In fact, Kennedy viewed appeasement as misunderstood by the general population, and especially the tale of Munich. The British mistake at Munich was not so much a diplomatic collapse, he once wrote, but rather a failure to provide military assistance to the Czechs at a critical time.[21]

America, the young president thought, could avoid Munich-like conferences over a thorny problem like Vietnam through rapid military assistance to the Saigon regime. Since diplomatic conferences did not imply American surrender in the cold war, Kennedy made it a point to pass along the following comment to the press preceding talks with communist leaders: "Let us never negotiate out of fear, but let us never fear to negotiate." This catchy phrase could even win him support from internationalists, like former Democratic presidential candidate and U.N. ambassador, Adlai Stevenson. Stevenson never wavered from his belief that tensions must be eased through cooperative diplomacy with the communists.[22]

It was a delicate game, and Vietnam watchers were confused by Kennedy's intentions. Britain's conservative periodical *The Economist* worried that the young president's tough talk about cold war victory eliminated any peaceful solution for all of Southeast Asia. Kennedy's approach, the editors complained, "bypassed one possible line of compromise after another," leaving the White House with the two sad options of "retreat" or "nuclear devastation."[23] This perception of Kennedy decision making constituted an irony to the approach Kennedy employed and preferred to leave as a positive legacy. The Kennedy team enjoyed assessing and analyzing dozens of policy options for Vietnam. The intellectual banter over Vietnam possibilities, Ted Sorensen remembered, made cabinet discussions exciting affairs, even though the banter was more exciting than the possibilities.[24]

Frederick E. Nolting, who served as a Kennedy ambassador to Vietnam, disagreed with *The Economist's* conclusion that Kennedy was a cold war/Vietnam extremist. He also would never share Sorensen's nostalgia with academic-styled analysis in difficult policy problems. Nolting recalls a cautious Kennedy who knew the difference between campaign rhetoric and triggering World War III. Yet, he also recalls a Kennedy who refused Ambassadorial Corps involvement in Vietnam policy-making, and that he turned a blind eye to reality. Kennedy, Nolting once noted, "refused to understand that the elected constitutional government of Vietnam was the best available."[25]

Nolting argues that Kennedy did little to sustain and support the Diem regime. Instead, his administration resigned itself early to support for a military coup. Corrupt and forever struggling, the Diem government simply was not liked by the Kennedy team. According to Nolting, Kennedy engaged in a reckless search for leadership more acceptable to his tastes.[26] Just two weeks before Kennedy's own assassination, Diem would be killed in a CIA-supported coup led by the South Vietnamese military. The consequences were poorly measured, for Kennedy believed that the best man and best government would emerge through American guidance. Since this guidance smacked of "Ugly Americanism," Kennedy, at the same time, worried about the total collapse of American influence in South Vietnam. He went to Dallas still wondering about Vietnam's shaky future and the messiness of Diem's demise.[27]

Should the world's dominant power chart the deaths of Third World politicians? Kennedy had entertained killing Castro at the time of the missile crisis, but denounced Eisenhower's failed 1958 effort to kill Sukarno of Indonesia. Arthur Schlesinger, always a Kennedy confidant, believes that the president was contemplating an official anti-assassination policy when he died.[28] In short, Kennedy raised the assassination issue, even considered indulging in it, but never resolved it.

Confusion always reigned over Vietnam. As early as April 1961, Kennedy aides McGeorge Bundy, George Ball, and Ted Sorensen pronounced Vietnam policy making in a chaotic state, more associated with American dreams for the region than practical policy. On April 28, 1961, the National Security Council (NSC) concluded that "we need a more *realistic* look" on Vietnam, hoping that "look" would emerge before the end of the year rather than by the end of Kennedy's first term. Nevertheless, the NSC still believed that time was on America's side to win the cold war in Vietnam.[29] By late 1963, there would be doubts on that point and Kennedy shared them, but it remained a matter of adjusting policies. America was still invincible to the Kennedy White House. Figuring out the mechanics of an invincible policy belonged to the second Kennedy term.

In 1961, the foundations for what was hoped would be an invincible policy had been laid. "There is no time-table," the NSC's Special Vietnam Task Force had continually stressed; however, they anticipated a working pro-American government in South Vietnam, happily supported by its citizens and at peace, by 1964. They were apologetic over a prediction that appeared so far ahead to fellow eager, young New Frontiersman. First of all, they recommended only one commitment, and it involved a slow-moving (for U.S. domestic political consumption reasons) "military buildup." South Vietnam, they insisted, accorded Washington a military foothold in "Southeast Asia proper" that signaled the correct anticommunist message to the region. The economic aid commitments could be adjusted as needed. A "joint plan" of economic reforms would downplay "Ugly American" backlashes, and a special negotiating team of Kennedy cabinet-level politicians and economic experts would begin work immediately following the personal introduction of this procedure to Diem by Vice President Johnson. Finally, the well-intentioned, but "misguided" long-range economic plans for Vietnam by the United Nations and other international organizations had to be intercepted and eliminated by Kennedy administration efforts. Internationalism would only slow the process of American cold war victory and lead to too many conflicts in aid distribution.[30]

The NSC admitted that Vietnam "cannot be saved unless it saves itself," but American could ease the salvation process.[31] In public, on the other hand, the Kennedy team remained conscious of "Ugly American" concerns and avoided talk of salvation and guidance. In May 1961, for instance, during a conference on the future of Laos, Secretary Rusk explained that "we are not here to try and impose an external judgement in a complex society—a society which in its origins derives from so many aspects and cultures of the Far East."[32] The same would be said of Vietnam.

Wracked by a civil war which pitted anti- and pro-communist factions against each other within one royal family, Laos was viewed by the White House as a more manageable situation than Vietnam.[33] Touting Britain's success in negotiating an end to the bloodshed in postcolonial Malaya nearly a decade earlier, Prime Minister Harold Macmillan had persuaded Kennedy to try some careful diplomacy over

Laos. A self-described "scholarly conservative," Macmillan was an old friend of Kennedy's father and had been labeled England's Eisenhower by critics of his slow-moving government. Macmillan believed that a coalition government of democratic and communist factions in Laos would keep the peace there.[34]

Less divisive in politics than Vietnam and considered by Westerners a "gentle culture" in contrast to its neighbors, Laos could serve as a foundation for Southeast Asian peace. "Inevitably," that peace would pressure Vietnam into the same condition. It was wishful thinking, but, after the Bay of Pigs, Kennedy wanted to look more successful at diplomatic gestures and less reckless in military matters. Macmillan's plan was appealing to him, and, since the British prime minister was admired by America's Republican party, Kennedy could wave the plan in the face of doubting Republican cold warriors.[35] "Munich" fears over inviting the communists to a coalition government were temporarily discarded. Supporting an arrangement whereby pro-American factions in Laos might lay down their arms first, Kennedy also proposed that pro-U.S. governments across Southeast Asia, especially the Diem regime, be prepared to dispatch troops to Laos within a U.N.-styled peacekeeping force.

The peacekeeping force idea, if necessary, would suggest pro-U.S. solidarity in the region, might isolate North Vietnam even further, and offer Free World respect to Saigon.[36] Yet, the Geneva negotiations over Laos would drag on more than a year to the summer of 1962. Any endeavor to demonstrate anticommunist peaceful intentions, from prisoner exchanges to outright halts to offensive operations, was usually met by accelerated procommunist military activity.

Despite detailed reports in reference to communist schemes to topple pro-U.S. regimes in Southeast Asia, including a report from his own vice president's fact-finding mission to the region in the spring of 1961, Kennedy worked with Macmillan's plan.[37] Through it all, Kennedy assumed that the enemy desired peace as much as America. He was wrong. Be it Laos or Vietnam, the enemy sought victory, not peace.[38]

Truly it was no easy task being the Free World's chief crusader. As always, Kennedy welcomed advice on complex issues such as Vietnam from a variety of intelligent sources. From the aging Douglas MacArthur, fired by Truman in the Korean War but still honored in the nation as an expert in Asian/Pacific warfare, Kennedy learned about the determination of guerrilla warriors in an Asian setting. MacArthur's support for American military disengagement in Vietnam was dismissed by Kennedy. Fearing that brushfire war would, at best, result in Korea-like inconclusiveness, or, worst of all, lead to nuclear confrontation with the entire communist world, MacArthur insisted that a nation dedicated to humane principles can certainly find a diplomatic alternative to war in Vietnam. Kennedy saw both MacArthur's respect for Ho Chi Minh's guerrillas and his fear of nuclear escalation as an exaggerated result of age and policy-making retirement.[39]

From Mike Mansfield, Kennedy learned that a politician can change his mind on anticommunist issues. Diem, Mansfield now believed, was beyond reform as was any alternative America could devise. A Buddhist-run government dedicated to ending the influence of medieval-styled landlords in the countryside and their corrupt tax schemes was the only answer, Mansfield said. Meanwhile, the United States could engineer an industrialization plan for Vietnam with SEATO member nation involvement. Mansfield's comments implied that this new Buddhist government must include pro-Ho Chi Minh activists in order to succeed. To Kennedy, Mansfield, as just one lone senator from Montana, enjoyed the luxury of changing his position. The president had no intention of giving up on established policy, thereby losing the support of cold war hardliners at home. If a coalition didn't work in Laos, it had no chance in Vietnam, Kennedy reasoned. The domestic hardliners would not tolerate experimentation abroad. Their vote was essential, he assumed, to his 1964 reelection chances. Many of these voters were Southern white males, and they were upset over Kennedy-supported civil rights reform. Kennedy could keep them only if he maintained his "pay any price" anticommunism, or so he thought. America liked innovative political leaders and "get moving again" activism, but there were limits. Reversing the "bear any burden" approach to the cold war, Kennedy believed, would be political suicide, not a lauded innovation.[40]

From the renowned economist and Kennedy ambassador to India, Professor John Kenneth Galbraith, Kennedy learned that Vietnam offered no investment returns to the United States. The country was hard to label strategic, and the Third World, including India, saw America replacing France as the new Indochina colonial. Promising a higher price tag than the Korean War, which in turn would alienate taxpaying Democratic voters, Vietnam was more trouble than it was worth. Despite Galbraith's new ambassadorial credentials, Kennedy saw no au-

thority in the economist's argument to comment on strategy. Economic
strains on the nation because of Vietnam stretched Kennedy's imagination, for economic indicators suggested endless growth for America's
worldwide economic influence in the 1960s. Hence, Galbraith's concerns were better suited to a Harvard classroom than to U.S. policy.[41]

Kennedy preferred listening and acting on the Vietnam advice of
in-house staffers, namely hardnosed intellectuals of similar age and
background who respected the president's determination to deal with
his self-imposed dilemma of cold war victory promises versus U.S. national self-interest realities. Roger Hilsman of the State Department's
Bureau of Intelligence and Research and Walt Rostow of the NSC were
two of Kennedy's chief advisors who fell in this category of mutual
respect. To Hilsman, the issue of communist insurgency in South Vietnam had to be resolved immediately through a counterinsurgency effort
led by American military advisors to the Army of the Republic of Vietnam (ARVN). Called "strategic hamlets," Hilsman hoped to link isolated villages, which supplied the recruits and supplies for the
communists, through civic and physical protection policies. The Vietnamese villages opposed their medieval-styled ties to landowners associated with the Diem regime. Hilsman's "strategic hamlets" proposed
to end this feudalism through direct U.S. involvement at the village
level.[42]

Kennedy hoped Vietnamese villagers would turn to Diem, or, most
likely, to a more reform-minded successor, as soon as Saigon demonstrated that it truly cared about its villagers. That caring could be demonstrated through support for the "hamlets" program. Rostow assured
Kennedy the caring and support would emerge if the White House
"imposed a Marshall Plan" on the Saigon regime. The president favored
a low key and less expensive effort. Rostow even preferred a maximum
number of U.S. military advisors, between five thousand and twenty-five
thousand dispatched over a two-year period. The Pentagon believed
more were required and Kennedy wondered if they were right; however,
he concluded by late 1961 that a large U.S. military presence might
encourage a larger North Vietnamese infiltration and even Chinese involvement.[43] More than seventeen thousand U.S. troops would be in
Vietnam by late 1963.

To Kennedy, North Vietnam was a nuisance rather than a threat.
Ho Chi Minh's government continued to totter on the brink of disaster
following a rice famine lasting several years. His aging political col-

leagues were more comfortable fighting battles of liberation against Japanese and French occupation forces. They resented bureaucratic tasks that provided little revolutionary glory. Through infiltration, North Vietnamese cadres could offer advice and military hardware to select opponents of Diem. Yet, the real test of strength, Kennedy believed, involved the South Vietnamese opposing communist inroads within South Vietnam itself. Despite Ho's antiimperialist popularity even in South Vietnam, Kennedy still saw him as a tired revolutionary leading a struggling government. Only the continued corruption and general ineffectiveness of the Diem government would elevate, in contrast, the significance of Ho Chi Minh in the South Vietnamese public mind.[44]

But what if Ho did become touted as the George Washington of all Vietnam and even Southeast Asia? As always in Kennedy foreign policy decision making, a variety of options were entertained. In January 1962, the president and his Joint Chiefs of Staff (JCS) discussed the possibility of an all-powerful Ho and what to do if it happened. The JCS insisted that Kennedy must not be reluctant to use nuclear warfare in Southeast Asia. Although Kennedy expressed his usual doubts about Ho's potential for aggression, he did discuss the idea of nuclear assault on Hanoi under "special circumstances." He requested specific information concerning the proper procedure for ordering a nuclear strike in Ho's corner of the world. Wanting to streamline the authorization procedure in the interest of swift response, Kennedy rewrote the rules. A president, as of late January 1962, could launch a nuclear strike in the Asian/Pacific Third World without consulting the Secretary of Defense, the JCS, or regional allies. The job would be finished quickly; however, Kennedy still doubted it would be necessary in 1962. If so, it would be triggered by a North Vietnamese-led ground assault into neighboring countries. America's nuclear retaliation would be determined by the president alone under executive privilege priorities.[45]

Kennedy stood on shaky Constitutional ground with this executive privilege decision. Once informed by his older brother of the new nuclear option on Vietnam, Robert Kennedy, the attorney general, cautioned the president. "It is almost impossible to describe in general terms the situations in which a claim of Executive Privilege is justified," Robert Kennedy said.[46] Nuclear war over Vietnam might not constitute such a claim. Both Robert and John Kennedy agreed that Vietnam "probably" would not raise nuclear options. Both worried that the president might still be "forced" to cross the line of "can do" campaign rhetoric and drag the White House into a Constitutional crisis over both executive privilege and national security policy making.[47]

The Kennedy brothers' joint concerns did not mean the president was required to reverse his decision on a streamlined process for nuclear war. A clever defense for it had to be arranged if the situation arose. Formulating that defense was the problem, not the nuclear war process. Senator John Stennis (D-Miss.), who chaired a subcommittee on Defense Special Preparedness and was a conservative critic of Kennedy policies ranging from national defense to civil rights, was already berating the White House for keeping Congress too much in the dark on Executive branch decision making. Although a staunch cold warrior who would have, most likely, supported an anticommunist policy which led to nuclear confrontation, Stennis preferred the full Constitutional involvement of Congress in these major decisions. He also had his doubts that Vietnam was the right place to focus that confrontation. He remained more concerned about Western Europe/Eastern Europe tensions.

To the Kennedys, Stennis was a white Southern racist who feared that executive privilege would be used to justify domestic racial desegregation. Also given Stennis' strong anticommunist credentials, the Kennedys figured that Stennis wanted to reap the political benefits of being involved in cold war victory decisions. From their point of view, Stennis was an opportunist, but a powerful one who had to be answered. That answer would involve a deliberate link to Eisenhower's view of executive privilege, making the Kennedy approach a bipartisan tradition.[48]

During the 1954 Army-McCarthy Hearings when the Eisenhower administration charged Senator McCarthy with inventing treasonous charges against the Army Officer Corps, the president had refused to release to Congress all White House documentation that proved their case against McCarthy. National security priorities had been claimed, given the involvement of the Army in the era of the Korean War. Eisenhower's approach prevailed, although it was not loved by Congress or the press. Escalating tensions in the cold war would make claims of executive privilege easier to defend, Robert Kennedy concluded. Meanwhile, public opinion supported a swift end to the influence of communism in the world. Unassailable presidential power promised to get the job done.

The attorney general always urged caution when dealing with Stennis and always expressed worries over a potential Constitutional crisis in a nuclear war over Vietnam, but still urged his brother not to reverse his decisions because of these problems. Preferring firmness in the face of a potential congressional revolution over presidential war making, the president instructed his staff, as well as the Departments of State and Defense, "not to give any testimony or produce any documents which would enable the Senate's Special Preparedness Investigating Subcommittee to identify and hold accountable any individual with respect to any particular speech that he has reviewed."[49]

Stennis's Constitutional argument for "checks and balances" in warmaking decisions remained a frustrating one to the Kennedys. The conviction that they would prevail against this argument, if Vietnam even really escalated it, permitted them to soldier on. Although Presidents Johnson and Nixon are credited and castigated for employing executive privilege in Vietnam-related matters, the foundation was laid by the Kennedy White House. Moreover, it was laid in deadly reference to the nuclear destruction of North Vietnam, and without consulting a soul. But how serious were they? Secretary Rusk remembers endless late evening discussions on Vietnam and its neighbors, yet always in the context of being a minor, if not expendable issue. There was a sense of wasting time with a situation that would rectify itself with a minimum of U.S. assistance in a few years. Usually discussed after the "big picture" of U.S.-Soviet relations and NATO matters, Vietnam was an "end of the day" discussion.[50] This did not jive with the "bear any burden" rhetoric, and the Kennedy White House was aware of the contradiction. Although forever puzzling to the Kennedy administration, Vietnam was a management problem, nuclear options and all, within the larger cold war tale.[51]

Weary of growing Buddhist unrest, an apparent lack of will on the part of ARVN troopers to quell the communist insurgency, and headline-making stories of the corrupt Diem regime, Kennedy told the press in September 1963 that the South Vietnamese leader had lost touch with his people. Only "changes in policy and perhaps with personnel" would make a difference.[52] The announcement was followed by a cutoff in more economic aid packages, and a request that Diem's version of the Special Forces, controlled by members of his own family, must now follow the orders of the American-advised ARVN officer corps. To Diem, this was American imperialism. To the ARVN generalship, it signaled Kennedy support of a coup. To the CIA, a solidly pro-American, yet temporary ARVN military regime was preferable to the worn-out Diem. The generals would do better, or so the Kennedy team always had believed.

Through CIA contacts to Duong Van Minh, Diem's chief of the general staff and a coup advocate, the Kennedy administration informed ambitious generals that a military take-over was in the interest of both nations. In any event, Kennedy preferred to keep America's involvement in the coup a low-key affair. Any "Ugly American" backlash in the Third World, of course, was to be avoided. He got his wish. Few mourned Diem, following his murder in the coup of early November 1963. Planning an address to a potentially hostile crowd in Texas for the 23rd of November 1963, Kennedy intended to assure Democratic conservatives that America's determination to win in Vietnam, Diem or no Diem, continued with vigor. "Pay any price" politics demanded nothing less, even through early surveys from the U.S. Embassy in Saigon indicated widespread South Vietnamese distrust and disgust for their new government.[53] In fact, that government would fall to another military coup in less than 90 days.

NEW PACIFIC COMMUNITY

Throughout his administration, Kennedy had hoped for a solution to Vietnam, but those hopes had been linked to a larger dream, a plan for the entire Asian/Pacific region that would keep the peace for decades and stimulate great economic adventures. Kennedy envisioned a new era of Asian/Pacific cooperation stimulated by a new international organization. The New Pacific Community organization promised great rewards for the Kennedy administration's approach to national self-interest, and, of course, to the Kennedy career.

Devised between February and April 1961 by a personally involved Dean Rusk, his staff, and the NSC, the New Pacific Community plan was Kennedy's answer to campaign rhetoric that suggested he would win the cold war and eliminate the "Ugly American" at the same time through a new, "can do" Asian/Pacific policy. The plan was honed and first tested between April and November 1961. In a special "top secret" meeting in April 1961, Rusk assured his boss and the Kennedy cabinet that the New Pacific Community was a unique New Frontier program dedicated to the swift success of Kennedy foreign policy goals.[54]

Intricate and involved, Rusk's plan reflected the analytical powers, as well as arrogance, of enthusiastic New Frontiersmen. If the plan was accepted by the Asian/Pacific noncommunist governments, the complicated Vietnam situation, Rusk promised, would never arise elsewhere. Ideally, the plan's objective involved "stimulating democratic and economic progress in significant [to the U.S.] locations throughout the Pacific." [55]

No crisis or particular problem had compelled Kennedy to move in the direction of a Pacific League of Nations. Especially in the early months of his administration, Kennedy had examined all the foreign policies taken for granted by the Eisenhower administration. Pacific issues merited greater reflection from a major Pacific power, he had told his cabinet. Nevertheless, his refusal to accept expert advice on Vietnam did not represent the type of reflective, analytical policy decision that he often championed.

More to the point, the creation of the New Pacific Community, like Kennedy's support for the Macmillan plan, coincided with the Bay of Pigs. The Community was deemed a careful plan, whereas the Bay of Pigs clearly was not. Admitting that Pacific policy posed special problems for the Kennedy administration, Rusk assured the cabinet that the State Department was ready to assault the problem. The shape of the problem involved the struggle of "key" nations and territories to reach a high stage of political/economic development. Guam, the Trust Territory of the Pacific Islands, Indonesia, Australia, Japan, the Ryukyu Islands, and the Philippines constituted the "key" areas.

These nations, territories, and occupied islands were not simply picked at random. There were reasons for their stress in a new international organization, and most of them fell within two contingencies. First, America must be ready to champion its victory over the communists in Indonesia by actively assuring other Asian/Pacific locations of Washington's ongoing commitment to peaceful Third World development. Second, if American efforts in Indochina were bogged down, the United States would still have to be ready to focus its "full attentions" on neighboring Asian/Pacific locations. "Full attentions" meant shoring up strategic/defense ties with specific nations and territories, as well as initiating new economic assistance programs.

The State Department presented a scenario whereby certain areas of the Asian/Pacific region were prisoners of the cold war. The "side," American or Soviet, which appealed to these areas first would win their allegiance and, therefore, win the cold war in the Pacific. The matter of reviving or "upgrading" American policy in the Pacific remained a matter of successful "maneuvering" of select governments. The Eisenhower administration, according to the Kennedy team, preferred "raw confrontation" to "maneuvering." When it came to Pacific diplomacy, the Eisenhower White House, Rusk explained, "dealt with a real problem with unreal techniques drawing on questionable analogies."[56]

Considering the Pacific a "most vulnerable" area to communist penetration, Rusk noted that sufficient time and effort had been spent by Kennedy's predecessors to build an Asian/Pacific policy stressing Chiang Kai-shek's Taiwan and Mao Tse-tung's China. The former was secure, Rusk concluded, and the latter had been effectively isolated from world politics. A policy of vision was needed to include the "forgotten" but significant nations and territories of the region.

Japan, for instance, was one of these "forgotten" nations to be "maneuvered" in the interest of winning the cold war. J. Robert Schaetzel, the State Department advisor and analyst who had prepared the original New Pacific Community plan for Rusk, pointed out that no one nation or territory in his study required more urgent attention than the other. Rusk agreed. In the case of Japan, American-Japanese relations had reached a watershed. Japan's "exploding industrial society is vital to us," Rusk lectured his colleagues in the cabinet. "Because Japan is not closely associated with any Western entity other than the United States," the secretary recommended that Tokyo's interest in a healthy foreign trade relationship must be "cultivated" by the United States.[57]

With the position of the American military bases in Japan assured by treaty only months before Kennedy took office, the American government enjoyed a fine opportunity to downplay its lingering image in Japan as an occupying power. Although the American occupation had ended almost a decade earlier, the Japanese treaty of 1960 assured a continued presence by the American military. The specifics of the treaty had stimulated considerable anti-American sentiment throughout Japan. Rusk suggested that a new commitment to American-Japanese "economic cooperation" would extinguish this sentiment. It would also symbolize American friendship better than the Eisenhower stress on "joint American-Japanese distrust of the Soviet Union."[58] This happy working relationship had been a goal of General Douglas MacArthur's occupation administration. Its time had come, the State Department's plan suggested, promising that Japanese economic growth, enthusiastically supported and encouraged by the United States, would also meet the warm approval of Japan's Pacific trade partners.

Despite the glowing prediction of warm American-Japanese friendships and cooperation, there were specific matters that threatened it. One of the more controversial issues involved the future of the Ryukyu Islands directly to the south of Japan. Occupied by American forces following a series of bloody battles in 1945, the Ryukyus were also the home of Kadena Air Base, the Third Marine Division, and Toril Station Army base on the island of Okinawa. Japan claimed sovereignty over the island chain while America preferred the security of occupation.[59]

Hoping to defend their own unique culture, cultivate longstanding ties with Japan, yet take advantage of the American dollar, many Okinawans and other Ryukyuans hoped to play Washington off Tokyo.[60] Rusk urged that reason prevail in this complicated issue of conflicting interest. Indeed, as long as the rights of the locals were protected and American basing rights assured, the return of Japanese sovereignty appeared to be the wisest policy. It could demonstrate to all Pacific residents that America desired to bury the World War II past and that it had no "imperial designs" in the region.[61]

Demonstrating that American intentions were noble and not "ugly" in the Pacific remained, naturally, at the heart of the New Pacific Community effort. The Kennedy cabinet was particularly sensitive to charges of "hypocrisy" and "colonial tyranny" leveled against it by Premier Khrushchev. Khrushchev had made these charges during a 1961 speech directed against the new president and his alleged concern for international human rights. Khrushchev pointed out that the American-administered United Nations mandate over the Trust Territory of the Pacific Islands was the last of the post-World War II mandates still in existence. The Trust Territory, Khrushchev said, encompassed the size of the continental United States, and it remained the colonial preserve of Washington. How could Kennedy label Soviet policy imperialist, Khrushchev asked, when it was America that remained one of the world's most significant colonial powers? "Freedom to the American Pacific," Khrushchev exclaimed to the Western press.[62]

"If we are to succeed anywhere," Kennedy told his cabinet, "we must succeed in the Western Pacific."[63] To Kennedy, the Western Pacific was Micronesia, or the American Territory of Guam and the Trust Territory. According to Rusk, if Washington "terminated" the United Nations mandate and placed both Guam and the Trust Territory on the road to statehood or some other "permanent association" with the United States, the Khrushchev charges would be answered. More significantly, the image of the caring, noble America would be easier to champion throughout the Pacific region. To an extent, Khrushchev was right. The American presence in Micronesia carried embarrassingly strong colonial overtones in an era of Pacific decolonization. Boldly assuming that the islanders desired closer ties to the United States, Kennedy predicted statehood for the Micronesian islands by 1970.[64]

The nearby former American colony of the Philippines presented yet another challenge to Kennedy's New Pacific Community. Whereas Micronesia suggested a coming era of political and economic growth to the State Department, the Philippines appeared to be in a state of political and economic chaos. The problem might not be remedied by 1970, Rusk announced, but in the meantime, America could assure a secure presence for its large naval and air forces there by stepping up its economic and military munitions program. The Philippines still enjoyed a "competent infrastructure," Rusk noted, to support political and economic growth. All it needed was "further stimulus" from the United States. To the Kennedy cabinet, this "stimulus" would symbolize America's commitment to development in struggling Third World nations. Indeed, the image of the former colonial master helping the decolonized help themselves was attractive to Kennedy. He asked his cabinet to seek support in Congress for a dramatic boost in foreign aid to the Philippines.[65] But would the Philippines use the aid appropriately? Although he worried about the answer, Kennedy still favored aid.

Finally, there was the problem of Sukarno of Indonesia. Like the Philippines, Indonesia presented several difficulties to the Kennedy team in the realm of political and economic development. In contrast to the Philippines, Indonesia's problems were of a more serious, immediate concern to Kennedy. Obviously, there were areas in the Pacific, despite Rusk and Schaetzel's original opinion, that required urgent attention. Sukarno's government welcomed elements of the strong Communist Party of Indonesia (PKI) within it. Moreover, Sukarno's "Guided Democracy" rejected American-styled democracy, justifying strong-armed rule and a foreign policy of nonalignment. As Indonesia's most famous hero in the war of liberation against the Japanese and then the Dutch, Sukarno remained the symbol of stability in his impoverished nation. If Sukarno fell victim to a coup, retired, or died, Rusk warned Kennedy, the Indonesian leader's power base would be inherited by the PKI.

Dealing with Sukarno would never be easy for the Kennedy White House. The charismatic Indonesian leader enjoyed wide respect throughout Southeast Asia. The Eisenhower administration's efforts to topple him in the unsuccessful CIA-sponsored plot of 1958 only led to Sukarno's entrenchment, worsening Washington's "Ugly American" image in the Pacific. Rusk recommended a "meaningful dialogue" with Sukarno in the interest of: (1) stimulating economic development in Indonesia; (2) impressing all of Southeast Asia with America's peaceful intentions; and (3) assuring American economic interests in Indonesian oil, tin, and rubber. If successful in this difficult proving ground, the winning of Pacific region allegiances to the American side in the cold war might be quickly achieved. Thus, preventing communist growth in Indonesia was discussed by the Kennedy White House with the same type of concern that it discussed Vietnam.[66]

All of the problems in these "key" areas of the Pacific could be "managed" within a new and specialized international organization, or so Kennedy believed from the moment he first read Rusk's proposal. The work of the New Pacific Community would not conflict with the work of existing international organizations. Its role would be to plan and coordinate the economic development of the Pacific region as well as oppose communist growth. The nations stressed in Rusk's original study would play primary roles in the directing body of the organization. Essentially acting as referees, American representatives would always be present at New Pacific Community meetings. Rusk recommended Australia as its headquarters. The Australians, he pointed out, were the most successful, American-styled democrats in the Pacific region. With America's help, Australia could become the symbol of the best possible Pacific state, championing America's view of economic development and peace throughout the Pacific.[67]

Although American-Australian relations were warm, Rusk was not pleased with Canberra's reluctance to become involved in anticommunist causes, particularly in Southeast Asia. Australia would be flattered by its American-deemed "activist role" in the new organization, Rusk believed. It was only a matter of time, he said, before Canberra accepted its destiny as America's anticommunist partner in the Pacific.[68]

The precise mechanics regarding how the organization would be established, administered, and financed was, for more than two years, never a matter of serious concern for the Kennedy White House. "First step" diplomacy in this matter involved winning commitments from the "key" nations to accept memberships. Success on this point alone, Kennedy believed, would isolate North Vietnam and procommunist insurgents in South Vietnam as radical, bizarre, and not worth the political

attention of anyone in Southeast Asia. Wrapped in righteousness, New
Frontier "can do" optimism, and the confidence of American powers
of persuasion, the New Pacific Community, said its creators, promised
greatness. Details could be worked out later.

By late 1963, the New Pacific Community remained on paper and
the Vietnam situation might have been bizarre, but it was real. Kennedy
maintained vigorous negotiations with the "key" nations, urging New
Pacific Community memberships and the acceptance of destiny. He
failed, and apparently died confused over the reasons why. Prime Minister Robert Menzies of Australia, pressured by Kennedy for months to
accept the headquarters role for the New Pacific Community, summed
up the Kennedy effort by suggesting that the Americans hoped to make
Australia "the 51st state through their new organization."[69] All other
"key" nations made similar comparisons. Prime Minister Hayato Ikeda
of Japan, for instance, saw the proposed organization as a means to
stifle Japanese investment in the Asian/Pacific region, robbing Tokyo of
its dream for an aggressive economic foreign policy in the 1960s. The
New Pacific Community only furthered American economic dominance
in the Pacific, he said. He also complained that Kennedy's disinterest
in informing the Japanese government of daily events during the World
War III–threatening Cuban missile crisis foreshadowed a conniving and
dishonest America in the New Pacific Community organization.[70]

Did American power have limits? This was the larger question posed
by both Vietnam and the New Pacific Community plan and negotiations. By November 1963, a solution to Vietnam remained elusive and
the New Pacific Community scheme had been turned down by all potential members. Neither difficulty stimulated a review of 1961 New
Frontier goals in Asian/Pacific policy. The issue of limited American
power would be left to Kennedy's successors to accept and adjust.

ENDNOTES

1. NSC Task Force Report: "Plan for Vietnam," April 28, 1961, Box 34/Sub-
   ject Files, 1961–64 (Foreign Policy), Papers of Theodore Sorensen, JFK
   Library; See the opening chapters to John Hellmann, *American Myth and
   the Legacy of Vietnam* (New York, 1986), and Bruce Palmer, *The 25 Year
   War: America's Military Role in Vietnam* (Lexington, 1984); Stephen Pelz,
   "John F. Kennedy's 1961 Vietnam War Decisions," *Journal of Strategic
   Studies*, Vol. 4 (December 1981), pp. 356–385.

2. Schlesinger, *Robert Kennedy and his Times*, p. 96.
3. Paterson, et. al., *Kennedy's Quest for Victory*, pp. 21–22.
4. Rusk to Kennedy, February 2, 1961, POF/Box 111, JFK Library. See also Timothy Maga, *John F. Kennedy and the New Pacific Community* (New York, 1990), pp. 1–13.
5. *Ibid.* (last entry), pp. 111–115.
6. "The New Pacific," Collection of Speeches from Kennedy's 1960 swing tour of Pacific islands, August 1960, Senate Files, JFK Library.
7. Ron Nurse, "American Must Not Sleep: The Development of John F. Kennedy's Foreign Policy Attitudes, 1947–1960" (Ph.D. dissertation, Michigan State University, 1971), pp. 56–132; Kennedy to the Joint Chiefs of Staff, July 1954, Records Group 218/Congressional Correspondence, National Archives.
8. Eugene Black, president of the World Bank, to Kennedy (plus memo on "America's Attitude Toward the Underdeveloped World," May 8, 1956, and Kennedy speech: "America's Stake in Vietnam: The Cornerstone of the Free World in Southeast Asia," June 1, 1956, POF/Box 135, JFK Library.
9. Kennedy's lack of interest in the tasks of congressional representation, including the "mundane" concerns of business, is part of the opening material to Thomas C. Reeves, *A Question of Character: John F. Kennedy in Image and Reality* (New York, 1991). For the influence of groups such as the American Friends of Vietnam, see the "Incentives for Activism" section of Ronald B. Rapoport, Alan I. Abramowitz, and John McClennon, eds., *The Life of the Parties: Activists in Presidential Politics* (Lexington, 1986).
10. Kennedy speech, "America's Stake in Vietnam," June 1, 1956 and transcripts of the first annual conference of the American Friends of Vietnam, June 1956, POF/Box 135, JFK Library.
11. "Not Forgotten," Kennedy speech submitted to the record of the first annual conference of the American Friends of Vietnam, June 1956, ibid.
12. *Ibid.*; "Vietnam's First Friend" (Mansfield speech, June 1956), ibid. Archimedes L. A. Patti, *Why Vietnam? Prelude to America's Albatross* (Berkeley, 1980). Patti's volumous analysis examines the motivations and objectives of Ho Chi Minh and Diem before the commitment of American troops. "Of Course, Vietnam," Kennedy speech submitted to the record of the American Friends of Vietnam conference, June 1956, POF/Box 135, JFK Library. Ibid.; John P. Burke and Fred I. Greenstein, *How Presidents Test Reality: Decisions on Vietnam, 1954 and 1965* (New York, 1989), pp. 3, 289; H. W. Brands, Jr. *Cold Warriors: Eisenhower's Generations and American Foreign Policy* (New York, 1988), p. 211.
13. Uniqueness was important to Kennedy and to the Kennedy mystique. See the "Kennedy" chapter in Theodore J. Lowi, *The Personal President: Power Invested, Promise Unfulfilled* (Ithaca, NY, 1985).
14. Hebert S. Parmet, *JFK: The Presidency of John F. Kennedy* (New York, 1983), p. 354; William Manchester, *Remembering Kennedy: One Brief and Shining Moment* (Boston, 1983), pp. 213–214.
15. Vietnam policy papers/testimonies of Edmund Gullion to Senate Foreign Relations Committee, 1954, Conference Files/60-627, Department of State

Records Service Center; Richard Walton, *Cold War and Counterrevolution: The Foreign Policy of John F. Kennedy* (New York, 1972), pp. 202–234; William Rust, *Kennedy in Vietnam* (New York, 1965), pp. ix–xvii.

16. Quote from: Godfrey Hodgson, *America in Our Time* (New York, 1976), p. 233.
17. Robert F. Cuervo, "John F. Kennedy and the Munich Myth" in Harper & Krieg, *John F. Kennedy*, pp. 131–141.
18. Dwight E. Lee, ed., *Munich: Blunder, Plot, a Tragic Necessity?* (Lexington, Mass., 1970), p. 100.
19. Secretary of State Rusk even quoted from a 1960 Kennedy speech on this issue, and stated how, through new determined efforts, American diplomacy with communists had become more "secure" in the opening months of the Kennedy administration. See Rusk's introductory comments to the conference on Laos in Geneva, May 12, 1961, Box 51/Classified Subjects–Laos, Papers of Theodore Sorensen, JFK Library.
20. Rusk, "Reflections in Foreign Policy" on Thompson, ed. *The Kennedy Presidency*, pp. 190–201.
21. "A Dreamer Wide Awake," *American Heritage*, Vol. 16 (October 1965), p. 81. Kennedy's private attitude on appeasement contrasted greatly with his best public denunciation of "Munich," and that denunciation had been originally published twenty years before his presidency. See his: *Why England Slept* (New York, 1940). In 1960, he even warned publicly that appeasement would cost America "everything" from Indochina to the space race. See his: "If the Soviets Control Space—They Can Control Earth," *Missiles and Rockets* Vol. 7 (October 10, 1960), pp. 12–13.
22. See the copious Kennedy material in Craig Allen Smith and Kathy B. Smith, eds., *The President and the Public: Rhetoric and National Leadership*, Volume 7: *The Credibility of Institutions, Policies and Leaderships* (Lanham, MD. 1985), "The President and the World" sections.
23. "Before the Dead End," *The Economist*, June 24, 1961, p. 1343, Press Clippings Files, JFK Library.
24. Introductory comments to the Sorensen papers collection, JFK Library staff.
25. Frederick E. Nolting, "Kennedy, NATO, and Southeast Asia," in Thompson, ed., *The Kennedy Presidency*, p. 229.
26. *Ibid.* Searching for leaders acceptable to U.S. national self-interest is thoroughly justifiable according to Rusk. He advocated such searches throughout his foreign service career. See Thomas Schoenbaum, *Waging Peace and War: Dean Rusk in the Truman, Kennedy, and Johnson Years* (New York, 1988).
27. NSC report and review: "Current or Potential Problems in Asia," November 1963, NSF/Box 283–National Security Council: 11/63, JFK Library; "Situation in Vietnam," Classified testimony of Secretary Rusk and Roger Hilsman to the Senate Foreign Relations Comittee, November 5–December 16, 1963, *Executive Sessions of the Senate Foreign Relations Committee*, Vol. XV (Washington, D.C., 1987), pp. 899–915.
28. Schlesinger, "A Biographer's Perspective," in Thompson, ed. *The Kennedy Presidency*, pp. 21–25.

29. Bundy to McNamara, February 3, 1961, Kennedy to Bundy, February 6, 1961; McNamara to Bundy, February 23, 1961; and "Plan for Vietnam" (NSC), April 28, 1961, POF/Box 77–Defense, NSF/Box 328–Meetings, and Box 34 of the Theodore Sorensen Papers, JFK Library.
30. *Ibid.* National Security Action Memorandum No. 52, May 11, 1961; "Current or Potential Problems in Asia" (NSC report and review of 1961 events), January 11, 1962, Box 52/Classified Subjects of the Theodore Sorensen Papers, and NSF/Box 283–National Security Council: 1/62, JFK Library.
31. *Ibid.*
32. Rusk's opening statement to the conference on Laos, May 12, 1961, Box 51/Laos of the Theodore Sorensen Papers, JFK Library.
33. "Laos: Lessons for a New Look," Briefing papers for Secretary Rusk, Laos conference, May 5, 1961, ibid.
34. "Development of Laos through International Assistance," ibid. Situation in Laos and Vietnam," Classified testimony of Averell Harriman, Assistant Secretary of State for Far Eastern Affairs, to the Senate Foreign Relations Committee, February 20–27, 1962, *Executive Sessions of the Senate Foreign Relations Committee*, Vol. XIV (Washington, D.C., 1986), pp. 189–215.
35. *Ibid.* "Briefing on Public Attitudes on Major Issues" (Laos & Vietnam), Sorensen to Kennedy, July 11, 1962, Box 52/Classified Subjects of the Theodore Sorensen Papers, JFK Library.
36. "Southeast Asia Planning" (NSC record of meeting with Kennedy), August 29, 1961, NSF/Box 213a, JFK Library.
37. "Vice President's Visit to South Vietnam"–Foreign Affairs Discussion, May 8–16, 1961, NSF/Box 345, JFK Library.
38. Ralph B. Smith, *An International History of the Vietnam War*, Vol. 1: *Revolution versus Containment, 1955–61* (New York, 1983), pp. 224–225. Burner, *Kennedy*, pp. 74–75.
39. Rusk Briefing Papers (MacArthur) Laos Conference, May–June 1961, Box 51/Classified Subjects–Laos of the Theodore Sorensen Papers, JFK Library.
40. Mansfield to Kennedy, November 2, 1961; Schlesinger to Bundy, November 15, 1961; Ball to Bundy, May 1, 1962; NSF/Box 194, Box WH-19 of the Arthur Schlesinger Papers, POF/Box 88, JFK Library.
41. Galbraith to Kennedy, November 1961, POF, Box 128a, JFK Library.
42. "New Tasks for Our Armed Forces," Classified Defense Department report, May 12, 1961; National Security Memorandum No. 2 and McNamara report to Kennedy; "Development of Counter-Guerilla Forces," February 23, 1961; Hilsman to Maxwell Taylor, February 23, 1961; Hilsman to Maxwell Taylor, February 2, 1962, POF/Box 77-Defense, JNSF/Box 328-Meetings, NSF/Box 195, JFK Library. Hilsman, *To Move a Nation*, p. 438.
43. Mutual Security Program (Vietnam), Rostow Memorandum, February 22, 1961, NSF/Box 283-NSC, JFK Library.
44. Appendix A: "Situation in Vietnam," Classified correspondence between the Kennedy administration and the Senate Foreign Relations Committee,

Executive Sessions, Vol. xiv-1962, pp. 811–820; U.S. House of Representatives Committee on Armed Services, *United States–Vietnam Relations, 1945–67* (Washington, D.C., 1971), pp. 448–454.

45. JCS Report: "Alert Procedures and JCS Emergency Actions File," January 16, 1962; Carl Kaysen to Bundy, April 16, 1962; Robert Kennedy to the President, plus report: "Executive Privilege," February 8, 1962, NSF/Box 281, NSF/Box 373, Box 34 of the Theodore Sorensen Papers, JFK Library.
46. *Ibid.*
47. *Ibid.* For Kennedy's attraction to executive privilege claims over nuclear defense, see: Bernard J. Firestone, "Defense Policy as a Form of Arms Control: Nuclear Force Posture and Strategy under John F. Kennedy" in Harper and Krieg, *John F. Kennedy*, pp. 57–69; William Kaufman, *The McNamara Strategy* (New York, 1964), pp. 1–52; Fred Kaplan, *The Wizards of Armageddon* (New York, 1983), pp. 237–246.
48. "Senator John Stennis: A Profile, "Senate Historical Office Working Paper, 1990; "Executive Privilege," February 8, 1962; Kennedy to McNamara February 8, 1962; Kennedy to Rusk, February 9, 1962; Box 34 of the Theodore Sorensen Papers, JFK Library.
49. *Ibid.*
50. Dean Rusk, "Reflections on Foreign Policy," in Thompson, ed., *The Kennedy Presidency*, pp. 190–201.
51. See the "Kennedy" chapter in Richard E. Neustadt, *Presidential Power and the Modern Presidents: The Politics of Leadership from Roosevelt to Reagan* (New York, 1990), pp. 16–58, Thomas G. Paterson, "John F. Kennedy and the World," in J. Richard Snyder, ed. *John F. Kennedy: Person, Policy, Presidency* (Wilmington, DE, 1988), pp. 123–138.
52. *Public Papers of the Presidents: John F. Kennedy, 1963* (Washington, D.C., 1963), p. 652.
53. See the: "Washington: Vacillation and Betrayal" chapter in Frederick Nolting, *From Trust to Tragedy: The Political Memoirs of Frederick Nolting, Kennedy's Ambassador to Diem's Vietnam* (Westport, CT, 1988); Ellen J. Hammer, *A Death in November: America in Vietnam, 1963* (New York, 1987), pp. 284–285. Rusk and Hilsman testimony, "Situation in Vietnam," November 5–December 16, 1963, *Executive Sessions*, Vol. xv, pp. 899–915.
54. "Observations on Proposal for a New Pacific Community and Review of April Cabinet Sessions," J. Robert Schaetzel to George Ball, internal State Department memorandum and report, November 7, 1961, NSF/Box 345, JFK Library. See also Maga, *John F. Kennedy and the New Pacific Community.*
55. "Observations on Proposal," November 2, 1961, NSF/Box 345, JFK Library.
56. *Ibid.*
57. *Ibid.* Briefing Material: Visit of Prime Minister Ikeda, State Department to Kennedy, June 23, 1961, PDF/Box 120, JFK Library.
58. Herbert Kahn, *The Emerging Japanese Superstate* (Englewood Cliffs, 1970), chapter 2; "Observations on Proposal," November 2, 1961, NSF/Box 345, JFK Library.

59. Herbert Passin, ed. *The United States and Japan* (Englewood Cliffs, 1966), pp. 29–56, 73.
60. George Kennan, "Japan's Security and American Policy," *Foreign Affairs*, Vol. 43 (October 1964), pp. 14–28.
61. Briefing Material: Visit of Prime Minister Ikeda, State Department, to Kennedy, June 23, 1961, POF/Box 120, JFK Library. Akio Watanabe, *The Okinawa Problem: A Chapter in Japan-U.S. Relations* (Carlton, Australia, 1970).
62. For background, see the introductory material to Dr. Anthony Solomon to Kennedy, October 9, 1963: "Report by the U.S. Government Survey Mission to the Trust Territory of the Pacific Islands," Pacific Confidential Collections, Micronesian Area Research Center (MARC), University of Guam; "Observations on Proposal," November 2, 1961, NSF/Box 345, JFK Library.
63. *Ibid.*
64. Kennedy to McNamara, January 31 and February 1, 1961, Guam/Box 101, JFK Library.
65. "Country Data—Philippines (Background paper), Vice President's Visit to the Philippines, May 1961," NSF/Box 242. Smith, *An International History of the Vietnam War*, Vol. 2: *The Kennedy Strategy* pp. 136–137. See also the introduction to Edwin Reischauer, *Beyond Vietnam: The United States and Asia* (New York, 1967). "Observations on Proposal," November 2, 1961, NSF/Box 345, JFK Library.
66. *Ibid.* (last entry). Briefing Material to Kennedy-Sukarno Meeting, April 1961, and "Background to Plan of Action for Indonesia," State Department, October 2, 1962, NSF/Box 338, JFK Library. See also the memoirs of Kennedy's ambassador to Indonesia: Howard Jones, *Indonesia: The Possible Dream* (New York, 1971); and Timothy Maga, "The New Frontier vs. Guided Democracy: JFK, Sakarno, and Indonesia, 1961–1963," *Presidential Studies Quarterly* Vol. xx (Winter 1990), pp. 91–102.
67. Rusk to Kennedy, February 2, 1961—NSC Briefing Papers for Kennedy on Meeting with Prime Minister Menzies of Australia, February 22, 1961; "Observations on Proposal," November 2, 1961, POF/Box 111 and NSF/Box 345, JFK Library.
68. *Ibid.* (last entry); State Department Memorandum: Current Status of U.S.-Australian Relations, March 14, 1962, POF/Box 111, JFK Library.
69. Kennedy-Menzies Meeting, June 20, 1962; Kennedy to Menzies, August 19, 1963; Status of U.S.-Australian Relations, November 1963, NSF/Box 6, JFK Library.
70. Rusk to Reischauer and Kennedy to Ikeda, July 25, 1963; Ikeda to Kennedy, July 31, 1963, POF/Box 120, JFK Library.

CHAPTER 5

The "Four Dilemmas": Berlin, Africa, Free Trade, and China

Recalling a happier day nearly thirty years earlier, Pierre Salinger, Kennedy's White House press secretary, once noted that his boss found it difficult "to prove his real worth in the most powerful office in the world."[1] Frustrating problems which grated the nerves often stood in the way of laying the groundwork for the New Frontier's better world. In the realm of diplomacy, Kennedy told Salinger in October 1963, he wished "four dilemmas would simply resolve themselves."[2] He had bigger fish to fry.

A hardline response to Khrushchev's construction of the Berlin wall threatened World War III and, hence, brought on one dilemma. Yet, the wall remained, and even New Frontier champions, such as Senator William Fulbright, chairman of the Senate Foreign Relations Committee, wondered if Americans were willing to die for Germans who were only 20 years earlier killing U.S. troops by the thousands. Kennedy wondered too.[3] Next, there was Africa. Decolonizing faster than the mapmakers could keep up, Africa always troubled the Kennedy team. Could the New Frontier ever appear more appealing there than Communism or even nonalignment? Kennedy was not sure of the answer, and he hoped the already strong U.S. influence and presence in the Far East would serve as a precedent for success in Africa.[4] Easing trade restrictions against Japan and other nations was the third dilemma, for the "politics of free trade" alienated too many members of Kennedy's own party. Keeping allied solidarity against the diplomatic recognition of "Red China" was the last of the announced "Four," and it was becoming more trouble than it was worth. By the end of his presidency, Kennedy saw little hope in influencing developments associated with any of these four problems.

BERLIN

Kennedy's finest hours, like those of his successors, rooted U.S. foreign policy in pure self-interest. He canonized West Berliners as saints of freedom, proclaiming: "Today, in the world of freedom, the proudest boast is 'Ich bin ein Berliner.' " In any event, his confrontation with Soviet tanks in that divided city during 1961 was over America's power and presence in postwar Europe, not the fate of suffering West Berlin. He was prepared to "pay any price" when fundamental American interests were at stake, and Khrushchev became most aware of the fact. On the other hand, in the four areas that Kennedy bemoaned with Salinger, fundamental interests were never easy to define for the president. Given its threats of nuclear war, the Berlin issue was especially difficult to define.

Berlin represents "the testicles of the West. Every time I give them a yank, they holler."[5] This was Khrushchev's conclusion, although his Berlin policy involved more than just watching Americans squirm. Since the end of World War II, the Soviets wanted their old wartime allies out of Berlin. The allied presence there constituted, in Moscow's view, a dagger near the heart of Soviet Eastern Europe. Two weeks before Kennedy's inaugural, Khrushchev told the press that "peaceful coexistence" would become a happy reality in the 1960s, but "after Berlin was resolved."[6]

Khrushchev's solution, outlined in correspondence to the West German government, involved Free City status for Berlin. A Western refusal to negotiate that status would force him to make a separate deal with the East Germans over occupation rights. If the Western allies attempted to strengthen their military positions after a Soviet–East German deal was resolved, war, he warned, would be a likely result. A Berlin free of Western influence would impress Khrushchev's Stalinist critics, permitting him to concentrate on the economic reforms he had promised Soviet citizenry several years earlier.[7]

Khrushchev made his Berlin position clear to Kennedy when they met in Vienna during June 1961. A special treaty which once-and-for-all concluded World War II and recognized Soviet interests in Berlin was overdue, Khrushchev stressed, and war would indeed result if America marched across East Germany to defend the Berlin status quo. Kennedy countered, explaining that an American agreement to a fully Soviet Berlin would be raw, Munich-styled appeasement, an insult to Washington's allies and to the people of "free" Berlin, as well as a suggestion that America was retreating into isolation.

Trading childlike barbs, Khrushchev claimed to be the only real peacemaker in Vienna, while Kennedy made the very same claim. Both said their positions were irreversible, and they warned each other that death and destruction lay ahead in the near future. Kennedy saw Khrushchev as a crafty country bumpkin. Khrushchev saw Kennedy as an inexperienced politician and professional rich-kid-turned-president. Both stereotypes were rooted in fact, and both were presented with the dilemma of confronting humiliation in the face of allies and domestic critics versus having the "courage" to accept millions of casualties in a nuclear war.[8]

It was an unhappy state of affairs. "Why won't it go away?," Kennedy asked his cabinet in July 1961. The president was convinced the Soviet premier wanted to embarrass and destroy him, and that that desire carried equal weight with Khrushchev's other policy concerns.[9] Full military preparedness was essential, Kennedy concluded, but Moscow was also informed that a peace settlement was still possible. In practical terms, this meant a special congressional allocation of over $3 billion for Berlin defense, Reserve and National Guard unit mobilization, and a new fallout shelter policy for noncombatants in the States. Despite the war footing, all of this activity was also attached to a public pronouncement of "readiness" to negotiate. Expecting the worst, more than 25,000 East Berliners flocked to the Western zone in July 1961 alone. Politically wounded by the exodus, Khrushchev ordered a concrete and barbed wire wall to separate East from West Berlin in less than a month.

Although it did not appear to be the case in public, the crisis had ended with Khrushchev's Berlin wall decision. Anticommunist rhetoric flared from the White House over the wall's construction, and Kennedy's critics urged American action to tear down this new symbol of communist tyranny. Privately, the Kennedy White House breathed a sigh of relief over each brick Khrushchev put into the wall.[10] It meant the Soviet premier accepted the reality of an East and West Berlin. There would be no war. An allied effort to tear down the wall would resurrect the crisis and, most likely, trigger that war. Hence, nothing would be done.

Doing nothing created certain political dangers for a cold warrior. Kennedy dispatched an armored division from West Germany through Red Army territory to Berlin in order to demonstrate "U.S. commitment," test Khrushchev, and enlighten domestic critics. Those critics, including possible 1964 election rival Senator Barry Goldwater (R-Arizona), remained skeptical of Kennedy's cold war mettle, and the president acknowledged to his staff that a tough Berlin policy would have to be devised sooner or later.[11] In the meantime, Khrushchev's action more or less admitted his lack of influence in moving the White House to see things his way. The Soviet premier now enjoyed the opportunity to stabilize the East German regime, halt the refugee flow to the West, and improve upon Soviet–Eastern Europe relations. In that way, he achieved some bottom-line objectives, and a dialogue, although it produced little, continued between Washington and Moscow. Kennedy, at the same time, was duty-bound via Cold War domestic realities to assail the wall's construction. The rhetoric remained harsh and political mileage was gained through a Kennedy visit to the wall; however, the real influence of the Berlin crisis could be seen in McNamara's efforts to reform allied defense policy in Europe.

Criticized by the Pentagon as a humorless workaholic—too young (forty-four) for his new job and too much the product of the Harvard Business School and Ford Motor Company management—McNamara ignored the flak and considered the post-Berlin crisis period an excellent opportunity to downplay nuclear options in Europe.[12] He now favored a heavy stress on conventional forces defense. Telling the president that America needed a "flexible response" to Soviet threats in Europe, McNamara recommended a building-up of NATO forces. His position smacked of a certain cold war heresy. Throughout the 1950s, both American political and military leaders assumed that, given the huge land armies of the Warsaw Pact, any war in Europe would be resolved through a nuclear strike by the outnumbered NATO allies. McNamara's suggestion might not result in NATO forces matching Warsaw Pact forces man for man, but it did send an obvious message to Moscow. The United States favored resolving any armed conflict in Europe via conventional means. Toning down the cold war was the primary objective here.

French President Charles DeGaulle complained that McNamara's proposal constituted an American retreat from European defense.[13] The message to Moscow, DeGaulle said, was a defeatist one: America would use nuclear weapons only in the defense of American soil. Both McNamara and Kennedy had believed that European leaders would welcome a backing away from nuclear threats, and that the complaints would involve the arrival of tens of thousands of more American troops in NATO countries and larger conventional force commitments on the part of NATO. Instead, with DeGaulle acting as chief lobbyist for an organization he had bolted several years earlier, the Western European governments insisted that America maintain its status quo military obligations and not "overreact" to crises such as Berlin or the Cuban missiles matter.[14]

Kennedy had supported his defense secretary's approach, even though a conventional force buildup would cost the taxpayer more money in the upcoming 1964 election year. The voters supported less and not more nuclear threats, he believed. Western Europe's rejection of McNamara's plan came as another great surprise to the Kennedy White House, and Kennedy grew annoyed at the "let the Americans do it" attitude of Western European defense policy-makers.[15] Allied disagreements over defense, he concluded, only aided the Soviet cause. Conceding defeat of the "flexible response" hope in early 1963, Kennedy, like a parent scolding a child, castigated the Western European heads of state as obsessed with "prior prejudice, memory and rhetoric." He did so in a private, top-secret letter to each of them, noting that Western Europe has an obligation not only to defend itself but to assist America in anticommunist policies around the world.

> It is my opinion that we must continue to work, Europe and the United States, together not only for our well being and prosperity but for the hundreds living in the southern one-half of the globe whose poverty and hardships make them immediate present targets of the communist advances. Until Europe and the United States continue to work together throughout the world for the maintenance of freedom we will not be worthy of our historic responsibility. This is then my response for the battle is still waged seeking to divide the unity of the west.[16]

To some, Kennedy's comments implied that Europe had an obligation to assist America in volatile Southeast Asia should a major war develop there. To others, the president was acknowledging the difficulty of winning the cold war not only in Europe but in even more trying locales, namely Africa. The latter perception was closer to the mark.

AFRICA

In the early days of the New Frontier, Kennedy admitted to the cabinet that African affairs were "baffling" and a possible "no-win situation." Kennedy rhetoric praised African independence, and his Special Protocol Service, largely devised to welcome and assist incoming African diplomats, was new and a reversal of Eisenhower's concern for waning European power in Africa.[17] Yet, this did not woo African politicians away from communist or nonalignment attractions.

Happier African-American relations appeared to rest on America's backing away from strong connections to former European colonizers within Africa. That split remained a strategic impossibility, nor was it deliberately sought in the name of African dialogue. African political rhetoric in that regard was unwelcome at the Kennedy White House, largely because it was totally unexpected at first, and because it always played into the hands of the Soviets.[18]

Undersecretary of State George Ball declared Africa the "real quagmire" of the cold war. Southeast Asia had less political factionalism, less social bickering, and more American influence, Ball said, suggesting that Vietnam was child's play in contrast to African affairs. In 1961, Ball attempted to devise a general African policy for the president. The complexities of decolonization and tribal rivalry were reduced to the easier to manage scenario of communist versus capitalist confrontation. It was also easier to view African problems within a continental policy, thereby ignoring all the political jousting within each emerging small nation.[19]

Not taking a continental view had already put Kennedy in trouble. In February 1961, just days after taking the oath of office, Kennedy had announced an Algerian policy. DeGaulle's request for U.S. support against communist rebels in Algeria was denounced by Kennedy as a ruse to win American endorsement of a nineteenth century–styled colonial war against Algerian freedom fighters. Kennedy's attitude confused rabid anticommunists who reminded the president of his "pay any price" inaugural pledge. It was praised by liberals who believed that America had become too much of the sucker for anticommunist causes, and who saw the possibility of a precise, pro-independence, country-by-country policy developing for African affairs.[20]

Ball thought Kennedy's Algeria announcement had raised too many embarrassing questions about the mechanics of New Frontier foreign policy. Algeria was the wrong place to stress America's African concerns. Black Africa, and especially the future of the Congo, Africa's biggest dilemma, was the appropriate focus for America's attentions, Ball stressed. Success there would translate into cold war victory sooner rather than later, and the Democratic party's most loyal faction, black America, would be most rewarding at the polls.

Kennedy remained unmoved by Ball's assertions, but the Congo became the White House's African concentration.[21] To Kennedy, Africa was always a cluttered political map with dangerous pitfalls in the path of American intervention. Whereas Ball took it upon himself to see the cold war through to victory in Africa, no matter what it takes, Kennedy maintained a cautious, pragmatic attitude. By attaching American objectives to U.N. operations in the Congo, the Kennedy team would look very pro-Third World and, if the United Nations failed in its efforts to keep the peace in the Congo, the United States would still have been associated with a noble endeavor. It could enhance America's anticolonial, pro-independence image elsewhere.[22]

If Moscow established a firm presence in the Congo, Ball urged a military expedition to dislodge it. Kennedy did not see this African-Soviet headquarters emerging, and he did not believe the American people would want to sort out the factional politics of the Congo in favor of military action.[23] The Congo's cast of political activists was a long one. When Kennedy took office, President Joseph Kasavubu, in charge of the Congo's central government, had arrested the region's eloquent and committed independence leader, Patrice Lumumba. Although Lumumba was the legitimate premier and defense minister, Kasavubu offered him a job as a minor policy-maker in his own government. In mineral-rich Katanga Province, Moise Tshombe maintained a separate regime in defense of the central government, and in Stanleyville, the Soviets had recognized the government of Antoine Gizenga, a Lumumba supporter. In the midst of the political jockeying, a U.N. peacekeeping force, dispatched in 1960, stood to protect Belgian citizens and property from social/revolutionary violence and looting. Lumumba, meanwhile, rejected Kasavubu's offer and was assassinated because of it.

Greed, power, tribal rivalries, and clashing egos helped characterize the struggling Congo politicians. Lumumba's stirring socialist rhetoric had, shortly before the end of the Eisenhower administration, led this self-appointed spokesman for the Congo to ask the Soviets for aid. The episode prompted Eisenhower's support for his "removal," including assassination if required. Kasavubu's house arrest of Lumumba saved the latter from a CIA hit squad, but his later assassination without CIA instigation did not assist U.S. policy. The Congo's power struggles continued. Ball worried that Kennedy did not worry enough about the region, and Congo politicians began pro-American campaigns in order to win American assistance against other Congo politicians.[24]

Eased out of power by a CIA-supported candidate and former agent, Cyrille Adoula, Gizenga became an instant nonplayer in the Congo's high stakes power game. The Congo's parliament was offered bribes by CIA operatives to vote for Adoula. Yet, this still left Tshombe and his Katanga rebels. Clever enough to tailor his new political rhetoric to sound anti-Soviet and pro-American, Tshombe began a campaign to rid the Congo of "radicals," i.e., all who opposed him. Richard Nixon and other American conservatives offered speeches in support of his efforts, urging direct American aid to Tshombe's cause. Ball and Kennedy finally agreed that the situation went beyond the usually perceived capitalist versus communist confrontation. Tshombe, they concluded, was an opportunist and a potentially ruthless dictator. They now supported a continued role for the United Nations, and, in 1963, Tshombe's drive to power was thwarted. Nevertheless, the violence escalated.[25] For years after the end of Camelot, the U.N. force would also continue its desperate efforts to abate this violence.

Forever reluctant to commit troops and Southeast Asia–styled aid packages to the Congo or to African affairs in general, Kennedy kept Africa as a "dilemma" rather than a policy. The sense of urgency to remedy cold war challenges there was less than in the Asian/Pacific region, or so he concluded. At first, that conclusion was based on despair and confusion. By late 1962, it was based on amazing revelations from the Soviet side. In November 1962, Kennedy met with A. I. Mikoyan, the Soviet deputy premier, at the White House. A diehard anti-Stalinist and old friend of Khrushchev, Mikoyan had just returned from a tour of Africa. Much of their discussion stressed Cuba and the continuing threat for peace by Soviet long-range bombers stationed there. Still, a sense of post-Cuban missile crisis calm pervaded the discussions. Nuclear war had been avoided. The Moscow-Washington dialogue continued. Africa, Mikoyan told Kennedy, was lost in hopeless confusion. Nonalignment was more preferable to the recently decolonized than cold war loyalties. Local power struggles of a certain virulence were more common as well, implying that Africa was not yet ready to participate in the cold war.

The Soviets were not going to retreat from influencing African events, but Kennedy learned from Mikoyan that Moscow was struggling as hard with African affairs as Washington. Reassessing their policy objectives, the Soviets were slowing the competition for African Third World allegiance.[26] The Kennedy White House could concentrate elsewhere, and not worry over its immediate lack of an African policy. Time was on their side. Thus American confusion over how to respond to African decolonization was easily dismissed as a temporary but affordable problem.

FREE TRADE

Given America's unassailable military and booming economy, there was much that Kennedy could afford. The New Frontier stressed ideological confrontation overseas, not dollar diplomacy in Africa or some other hot spot. The politics of foreign aid would not resolve the African problem, and more to the point, economic diplomacy was not the crux of a cold warrior's mission. Few were attracted to New Frontier service because of its interest in economic foreign policy and what it might accomplish in Africa or elsewhere. Economic considerations were built into New Frontier priorities, but adventure, excitement, and swift action were supposed to characterize the Kennedy promise. Money matters were procedural. On the other hand, Kennedy remained at ease with the language of international economics. He could personally dissect balance of payments problems, discuss the inner workings of the International Monetary Fund (IMF), and talk convincingly about maintaining the dollar's dominance in world markets. Even though his own State Department preferred cold warriors to economists as foreign policymakers, economic advisors, such as Walter Heller, chairman of the Council of Economic Advisors, welcomed Kennedy's interest in dollars and cents. Truman and Eisenhower, Heller recalled, could not balance a checkbook.[27]

International economic issues, especially free trade, remained a weak

spot for the administration according to Kennedy himself. Making it
easy for Third World nations to market their goods in America was a
decent contribution to the cold war victory effort. Pushing that opening-
up process along was another matter.[28] The Democratic party, since the
early days of FDR, had been on record in its opposition to protectionism. Closing doors to the consumer heaven known as the American
market led to unnecessary international tension, said the Democratic
free traders. Kennedy saw a direct link between the anticommunist commitment of America's allies and the availability of the American consumer to them.[29]

Were there limits to free trade? Could Kennedy push his party too
far, and, if so, would the damage harm the larger ideological thrust of
his foreign policy? In spite of the dangers, Kennedy moved forward with
this economic arm of the New Frontier. Admitting to his cabinet in
1961 that he was not exactly sure what he was doing, the president
tried to assure his colleagues that poor Democrats could handle money
matters better than rich Republicans. It was a wry partisan joke, and
no one was confident enough to laugh.[30]

Since the early days of Secretary of State Cordell Hull's 1930s recip-
rocal trade agreements, Congress had leashed the president on tariff
negotiation matters. Hull's and FDR's reasoning involved a certain disgust for Herbert Hoover's high tariff policies. That disgust was hitched
to a desire for at manufacturing-based economy fitting the nation's
potential for postdepression economic growth. Nearly thirty years later,
that growth was obvious. Yesterday's enemies, namely Japan and Germany, were in the same position of great potential growth, as were
several other anticommunist allies. America, Kennedy believed, thanks
to an overwhelming economic superiority, had the power and the obligation to further the economic growth of the anticommunist alliance,
champion free trade, and bring profit to American business at the same
time. It was heady ambition, but typical of the "can do" New Frontier.
In the face of this ambition, it was still preferable to ignore economic
matters if any other issue could be discussed in cabinet meetings. Kennedy might have known the language of economics, but he preferred
the language of political confrontation.[31]

The Trade Expansion Act (TEA) of 1962 granted the president
greater powers over international economic policy than ever before, and
without Congress's consultation. The press and many New Frontiersmen paid little attention. Yet, it was a mammoth victory for executive

privilege, which Kennedy always touted as a positive development in the march to cold war victory. It was also a victory for basic free trade ambitions, for it reduced tariffs on goods, via presidential order, 50 to 100 percent. The stress was Europe, and the rhetoric of TEA downplayed German industrial savvy for fear it might stir lingering World War II animosities. Indeed, the socialist Harold Wilson of England and the ultraconservative DeGaulle of France provided most of the concern in Congress over European objectives. Despite their differing political pedigrees, English socialists and French conservatives complained that free trade could become a smokescreen for the full "Americanization" of Europe.[32]

George Ball, always the visionary, saw trade liberalization as more than a Good Neighbor policy for anticommunist allies. He saw it as a foundation for healthy economic relations with the Soviet Union. If Khrushchev was serious about responding to Soviet consumer demand, the United States should be ready to fulfill any need. In the long run, Soviet appreciation for U.S.-made products would translate into Soviet rejection of communism and demands for American goods. Dollars and cents, Ball theorized, would do the trick in changing Soviet minds about communism and capitalism. That change of mind, "the kiss of capitalism," would guarantee American victory in the cold war. Kennedy had no objection to this scenario; however, he did find it rather dreamlike and impossible to achieve during his projected two terms in office.[33] While discussing trade issues with Deputy Premier Mikoyan in 1962, Kennedy even mentioned the point to him. Mikoyan asked Kennedy if an active U.S.-U.S.S.R. trade relationship was possible now that the tensions over Berlin and Cuba had subsided. Kennedy noted that the tensions would never truly subside, and that a frenetic trade relationship would probably take thirty years.[34] Kennedy's prediction proved close to the mark.

Mikoyan had learned that the president's cold war victory commitments were not rooted in empty rhetoric. He saw "peaceful coexistence" leading to a modest U.S.-U.S.S.R. trade agreement. Kennedy had little interest in establishing a policy that would assist economic growth in the Soviet Union, yet he still saw merit in Ball's "kiss of capitalism" hopes.[35] Nothing would be done.

Free trade reforms enjoyed the support of Democratic party luminaries such as Wilbur Mills and Hale Boggs, powerful House committee chairmen. They believed TEA was a better achievement for Kennedy than decisive civil rights reform. Even some Republicans such as former Massachusetts politician and secretary of state in the waning days of the Eisenhower administration, Christian Herter, saw Kennedy luring support from Republican ranks on the free trade, make-money-abroad issue. Kennedy made Herter, an old political rival with a liberal slant in a conservative Republican party, the special representative for trade negotiations.[36]

Herter's job, with the blessing of both parties, involved finding even more export markets. With economic indicators promising endless growth by the late 1960s, Japan posed the biggest problem to American global economic interests, and Kennedy worried that his entire free trade stress might collapse in a debate with Japan and with Congress over Japan.[37]

Like the hope of cold war victory itself, the idea of free trade, leading to a global economy guided by the United States, involved considerable dreaming as well. To Prime Minister Hayato Ikeda of Japan, America preached free trade but kept full access to its domestic market away from his country. TEA was for Europe, protectionism was for "the little yellow ones" [Japanese]. Kennedy assured Ikeda that America welcomed a new trade relationship with Japan, and that the prime minister's racial complaint in reference to the matter was misplaced. Proving the point would, as always, be another matter, and Kennedy predicted that Japan's economic goals would become a bitter problem for America in the 1960s.[38] It was a problem, he said, that the cold war did not need, and it also promised unwanted tensions with Congress.

In 1961, Ikeda announced that Japan sought to develop its own distinctive role in international economics during the 1960s. Growing Japanese economic interest in Southeast Asia demonstrated that ambition. In the late 1950s, specific reparations deals with former Japanese-occupied territories in Southeast Asia opened the door to future investment. That future was complicated by Peking's interest in the region and by the fact that Japanese-Chinese relations remained weak. Efforts to improve the Peking-Tokyo dialogue in 1962 and 1963 were begun by both governments, but collapsed while mainland China contemplated its role in the deteriorating Vietnam situation. Meanwhile, as early as February 1961, the Ikeda government announced that Japan's postwar economic debts to America would soon be paid. Robert Kennedy, returning from a meeting with Sukarno in Indonesia, would personally receive that payment in 1962. Without question, Ikeda successfully championed the issue of Japanese pride and prestige. Although he never sought Japan's independence from American ties, a Soviet-Japanese trade agreement in 1962 indicated that Japan was truly serious about breaking away from postwar isolation.[39]

Ikeda's talk of a new Japanese economic order, his friendly bows to Soviet officials, and Kennedy's insistence that recent memories of U.S.-Japan tension over the Eisenhower-negotiated Mutual Security Treaty should be forgotten, did not sit well with Congress. Kennedy exaggerated the level of anti-Tokyo sentiment in Congress and exaggerated the difficulties facing Japan-U.S. economic ties, but he did not depart from his course of furthering those ties.[40]

Throughout 1961 especially, Kennedy was plagued by anti-Japanese and protectionist legislation in Congress. Always targeting Japan over all other nations, these measures noted Japan's growing dependence on an export economy. They also declared America's interest in economic self-defense before these exports posed a threat to U.S. domestic industry; i.e., protection from an "economic Pearl Harbor" was required.[41] Spearheading the congressional effort were two former Kennedy stalwarts, Representatives John Baldwin and Leo W. O'Brien. Both men accurately reminded Kennedy that he had never expressed any diehard loyalty to free trade at any point in his career. Indeed, Kennedy would be basing his Japan-related decisions and other free trade matters on the priorities of foreign policy making and not economic thought.[42]

Baldwin proposed legislation that required a modification of Executive Order 10582, forbidding the American government from purchasing any Japanese product for any of its agencies, including the military. Kennedy noted that the Buy-America Act already prohibited the government from purchasing foreign products unless the prices for domestic goods were "unreasonable." Executive Order 10582 was a procurement measure, largely devoted to modernizing government offices with the latest and best equipment. Kennedy saw the Baldwin bill as not only an open door to a protectionist era, but also an attack on executive order privilege. In a special message to Congress, Kennedy lashed out at the Baldwin bill, anti-Japanese opinion, and protectionism in general. "A return to protectionism," he insisted, "is not a solution. Such a course could result in retaliation abroad with serious consequences for U.S. exports and our trade balance."[43]

As the weeks went by, Kennedy's attack on Baldwin grew stronger. He accused the congressman of injuring American-Japanese diplomacy, harming executive-legislative relations, and dividing Democrats. He asked him to drop the cause.[44] Baldwin obliged, but his bill was quickly replaced by an even more obvious anti-Japanese measure. Representative O'Brien, a friend of Kennedy and an ally in all other areas of legislation, sponsored a bill "to observe December 7th each year as the day that will live in infamy." The bill suggested that a national holiday was required to honor the American dead of the recent Pacific War, noting that the president himself was almost killed in that conflict. Furthermore, the bill implied that the Japanese had not yet repented for the Pearl Harbor attack and other World War II actions. Anti-American sentiment in Japan was used as a fine testament to the fact. Kindness to Japan's export economy, the bill proclaimed, must not be forthcoming.[45]

O'Brien's bill was deliberately written to coincide with Ikeda's 1961 visit to the White House. Kennedy informed Congress that he would never support protectionism and anti-Japanese legislation. He reserved a special comment for O'Brien.

"I suppose that all of us feel the same about December 7, 1941. However, we are now trying to IMPROVE Japanese-American relationships, and I doubt that calling the Japanese names each year is calculated to achieve that purpose."[46]

Although it involved a slim margin, the O'Brien bill failed to win a majority vote. Meanwhile, Ikeda's visit to Washington prompted the usually anti-American *Asahi Shimbun* (Japan's most significant newspaper) to declare the 1960s "the era of new beginnings" for Tokyo and Washington. The reason for the euphoria involved a loosely defined Kennedy-Ikeda accord to create the Joint United States-Japan Committee on Trade and Economic Affairs. Kennedy did not tell the press what the precise duties of this committee entailed, but its very announcement symbolized the end of protectionism to the Japanese and the opening of full access to the U.S. market. Good New Frontiersmen believed that America would always enjoy, thanks to the Joint Committee, the opportunity to control the level of Japanese imports to the United States. The American market was secure. Edwin Reischauer, Kennedy's Japanese-speaking Harvard-scholar-turned-ambassador to Japan, stressed that point. "We have a unique opportunity," Reischauer told a receptive White House, "to improve over bilateral relations with Japan and to influence as well the entire course of Japanese domestic and foreign policy."[47] Reischauer's assessment was in keeping with the larger New Pacific Community idea, and, like the New Pacific Community, optimism and chauvinism reigned.

George McGovern, director of the Food for Peace program, did not have the time to contemplate the big picture. With the Japanese island of Hokkaido requiring tons of livestock feed due to the unusually devastating winter of 1961–1962, McGovern wondered if relief efforts involved his office or the new trade committee.[48] Kennedy had McGovern ship the grain, but the trade committee received the credit. Meanwhile, Ikeda continued to complain that "structural impediments" remained in the face of Japanese imports, especially for textiles. In 1956, Japan supplied 76 percent of all cotton textile imports to the United States. By 1962, that percentage had dropped to less than 19 percent. Ikeda wanted an immediate lifting of tariffs, and the Japanese Socialist Party even arranged Tokyo demonstrations against "American economic imperialism." Tired of dealing with demanding Japanese politicians, O. I. Hague, Kennedy' s chief representative on the trade committee, observed that "new beginnings" remained "pretty farfetched."[49]

Kennedy's answer was a new round of negotiations with the purpose of finding some sort of agreement. That agreement was reached on February 1, 1963, establishing a scaled-down and complicated tariff structure that, from the American view, benefited Japan.[50] The agreement also assisted other nations, such as the Republic of China on Taiwan. Hence, international competition did not promise an easy capture of the American market in textiles or other trade items.

Japan's opposition to all nuclear testing, to Kennedy's World War III threats in the Cuban missile crisis, to continued American sovereignty over the Ryukyu Islands, and to U.S. conventional forces escalation on Honshu, as well as distrust over American economic competition in Asia, did little to assist Kennedy and "new beginnings" dialogue with Japan on trade. Throughout 1963, Ikeda complained that Japan's balance of payments with the United States was more than $170 million in the red. America's interest equalization tax, Ikeda's Foreign Ministry pointed out, was anti-Japanese and doomed economic progress. The complaints and accusations annoyed Kennedy. Shortly before his assassination, he told his staff that, given the perils of the cold war, Japan's anxiety over trade issues was difficult to understand. He even told a group of visiting prefecture-level Japanese politicians that American-Japanese relations would always be "uncertain" because of trade matters, and that cold war confrontation should be the primary concern of any nation's foreign policy.[51]

Although tired of congressional bickering and Japanese complaints,

Kennedy could claim the best U.S. dialogue with Tokyo in many decades. The defense establishment there was secure, and the White House had bent over backward to meet Japanese economic expectations for the 1960s. Yet, the whole process of trade relations was viewed as a sideshow to matters of political and military confrontation with communism.

CHINA

In the Far East, the big picture never stressed the mechanics of economic policy. Instead, to Kennedy, it had to stress the forced isolation of the world's largest nation, China.[52] If they decided to do so, the communist Chinese could destroy the New Frontier's anti-"Ugly American" inroads throughout the Asian/Pacific region, or so Kennedy had believed. Raising the memory of the sudden involvement of "Red China" in the Korean War, Kennedy had campaigned in 1960 with the promise that America would always be ready to counter Chinese threats in the coming decade.[53] But what would the counterattack entail?

Even President Truman, during a time of war, had refused to carry the Korean conflict onto Chinese soil. World War III would have been the result. The best China policy, Kennedy reasoned, was none at all, i.e., U.S. and allied nonrecognition of Mao's China. The trick was keeping America's allies, particularly in the Pacific, from dealing with China. With the doctrine of nonrecognition entering its second decade, allied solidarity was crumbling. Kennedy rhetoric depicted Chinese communism as more radical and more frightening than the Soviet version. The commitment to containing this radicalism was linked to the success of his foreign policy. Despite both public and private rhetoric that illustrated the point, he still had no idea how to keep China on the outskirts of world diplomacy.[54]

As early as February 1961, Kennedy told his cabinet that he would prefer a rapprochement with China, but political realities prohibited it. The allies would have to wait for America's lead in that endeavor. Leashing the allies until the right moment would be a difficult task. Even talking about China was a straining endeavor. Joking with the cabinet about this predicament, he offered them all a cash bonus if other areas of conversation could be found.[55]

The cabinet often accommodated Kennedy by keeping China-related matters brief, but the allies were not that generous. Trailblazing the effort to break the allied nonrecognition policy was Australia's prime minister, Robert Menzies. The issue was at the top of his agenda when he met Kennedy for the first time in February 1961.

In spite of staunch Conservative party/cold war credentials, the veteran Australian prime minister asked for a thaw in nonrecognition, noting that he spoke on behalf of many U.S. allies. Growing pressure to recognize China from the Australian Labor party, and public opinion increasingly sympathetic to that pressure, had taken its toll upon Menzies' hard anti-China line.[56]

Hoping to delay any unilateral Australian action, Kennedy explained to Menzies, and with some imagination, that the White House was reviewing the China policy from top to bottom. Such comments were in keeping with the New Frontier image of endless action. He said any shift away from nonrecognition would have to involve careful negotiations with the Chinese Nationalists on Taiwan.[57] Indeed, President Chiang Kai-shek of the Republic of China (ROC) was suspicious of Kennedy's "new directions" theme during the latter's campaign and in his inaugural address. He was also nervous over the Menzies mission. Since his 1949 defeat by Mao and retreat to Taiwan, Chiang had enjoyed unwavering support from previous American administrations. The one exception to this support involved his plans to invade the Chinese mainland. Chiang restated his approval for nonrecognition, and with characteristic fervor, in time for the Kennedy-Menzies meeting.[58]

Chiang announced that the ROC might not need U.S. support and that it was ready "to go it alone" in military operations against Chinese communist positions in the Taiwan Strait. The time had finally come, he implied, for the "recovery" of the entire Chinese mainland. Chiang's comments expanded his official Double Tenth (October 10) statement for 1960, whereby he promised a Chinese mainland restored to Nationalist control by 1965. The ROC leader's comments suggested to the Kennedy White House a resumption of the Chinese civil war, but American worries in that regard were more than a decade old.[59]

To Secretary of State Rusk, Chiang's fear of Kennedy's potential overtures to the Chinese mainland might quickly force him into a military struggle for which he was ill-prepared. Three weeks before Menzies' visit, the Australian press was already speculating over an American-Australian overture to Mainland China. Rusk had received word that Chiang was deeply annoyed that Kennedy-appointed diplomats in Asian/Pacific posts were speaking of "two Chinas". Indeed, in a candid press interview, Adlai Stevenson, America's ambassador to the United Nations, had noted that the United States could "probably" do nothing if the debate continued to seat a Chinese mainland representative at the United Nations and unseat the ROC delegation. Meanwhile, Chiang was intrigued by reports of famine on the mainland, and also by tales of unrest due to failed economic reforms and an uprising in Tibet.[60] Rusk continued to worry that Chiang had found the right moment to strike, and that international perceptions of Kennedy's "new directions" had hastened his decision.

International perceptions of Kennedy rhetoric had unquestionably become a problem. Although Kennedy had no plan to do so, the allies anticipated a nonrecognition reversal. Just forty-eight hours before Menzies arrived, Kennedy quizzed the cabinet. Should America provide what the allies anticipate? It was obvious that Kennedy had no problem with nonrecognition, but it was a most frustrating policy. The China position papers that he received on the day of Menzies' arrival reflected that reality. Both the State and Defense Departments argued that America could not afford to continue blatant nonrecognition, nor could it afford detente. A middle ground was required, but they had no idea what that might be.[61]

During their meeting, Menzies was direct and to the point with Kennedy. Noting that support for the recognition of China extended beyond the Labor party, the Australian press, and concerned voters, he said that the matter had become one of economic self-interest and political survival. One million tons of Australian grain had been sold to China at the beginning of 1961, exciting the financial community in his country, and perking the interest of New Zealand, Canada, and even Japan. Australian business urged further Chinese connections, and Menzies believed that a formal Australian-Chinese thaw in cold war tensions would rescue his government from its "image of tiredness and do-nothingism." Kennedy retorted that an Australian abandonment of the hard line would also mean an Australian abandonment of Free World defense against Chinese communist expansion. China had not abandoned its expansionist goals, Kennedy pointed out. Consequently, Australia would also be recognizing Chinese aggression, increasing U.S. defense commitments in the Asian/Pacific region, and denying its treaty obligations to the Republic of China.

Menzies had obviously expected more of Kennedy. Instead, the president insisted that Menzies discover a different issue that might rescue his government from a weak political image.[62] This was not what the Australian prime minister wanted to hear. Kennedy was, nevertheless, aware of Menzies' disappointment. He promised his visitor that a new, "moderate" policy would be forthcoming, and that he would soon visit several Asian/Pacific capitals to champion it. With the press fruitlessly anticipating the announcement of a new American-Australian approach to China after this meeting, both Menzies and Kennedy were subjected to penetrating questions on the matter. Kennedy's answers were similar to his comments to Menzies; however, he said nothing about a proposed "moderate" policy.[63]

The U.S. Congress was concerned about what Kennedy was not saying, and called Secretary Rusk to testify in a closed session of the Senate Armed Services Committee. Rusk apologized for the misleading press reports, accurately noting that the Kennedy administration had never promised a shift from nonrecognition. Offering a long explanation and defense of the administration's thinking on the China issue, Rusk confused rather than enlightened Congress. The growing Sino-Soviet split, he said, was especially delaying a "revised approach" to China. Both Eisenhower secretaries of state, Dulles and Herter, had once claimed that doctrinaire disputes between Moscow and Peking would have little influence on United States policy, for American anticommunist commitments remained firm. The Kennedy administration, as Rusk attempted to explain to Congress, saw the Sino-Soviet split as worth exploiting in the interests of United States policy.[64] In any event, he failed to define either this exploitation plan or the "moderate" China policy, for he had no specifics to match the "new directions" promise.

Like Kennedy, Rusk considered the Chinese more "extremist" than the Soviets. When a curious Congress asked him to define "extremism," he offered plenty of examples concerning Chinese "treachery." In Ethiopia, the Soviets pursued an aid program. In nearby Somalia, the Chinese supported and armed "the most radical group in East Africa." In Laos, the Soviets, at the time of Rusk's congressional appearance, were debating a peace plan, while the Chinese refused to discuss it. Meanwhile, the Soviets proclaimed their interest in disarmament, while the Chinese preached more and better arms for purposes of world revolution. Rusk's depiction of China as a "dangerously radical nation," willing to destroy a major symbol of Asian democracy, India, over "common border complaints," constituted a final State Department salvo against a full rapprochement with China.[65]

To Democratic Senator Stuart W. Symington of Missouri, a one-time rival of Kennedy in his presidential bid, Rusk's comments were hollow and contradictory. A majority of the Senate Foreign Relations Committee shared Symington's concerns. Republican Senator Alexander Wiley of Wisconsin thought that "moderate nonrecognition" was an unrealistic and unattainable goal. Would it involve a calming of tensions in Asia, he asked Rusk? The secretary had no answers. Democratic Senator John Sparkman of Alabama and Republican Bourke Hickenlooper of Iowa found Kennedy's efforts to support the ROC delegation's right to remain seated at the United Nations, while embarking on a new, "moderate" China policy, "unusual." Finally, Senator Hubert Humphrey, another Democratic rival of Kennedy's in the election campaign, admitted that the search for a "moderate" China policy would be difficult, but Congress must not obstruct the White House's endeavors.[66]

Humphrey's comments implied that Congress was willing to permit Kennedy a period of grace to find that elusive moderate policy, but that if the president's efforts failed, they would give him little solace. Failure, of course, was not part of Kennedy's political vocabulary. The "moderate" China plan became wedded to the mission of the New Pacific Community organization. A bold, innovative China policy would remain too risky for domestic political consumption, and the community approach permitted the Kennedy team to avoid the frustrations of dealing with the "two Chinas" within one new China policy.[67] The community worked with the concerns of a variety of Asian/Pacific nations at one time and with America's subtle guidance. It would be easier to manage the China dilemma within that framework.

In a decade's time, the New Pacific Community's tireless dedication to Asian/Pacific infrastructural development, various cooperative ventures, and democratic dialogue were expected to isolate Chinese influence as violent and imperialist. Replacing the "Ugly Chinese" image in the Asian/Pacific Third World was a major goal of the new organization. Convincing Chiang, and even American public opinion that it would work, was, again, something else.

Chiang doubted that a new Pacific organization would reject an accommodation with "Red China," given the right circumstances. He therefore remained suspicious of the term "moderate nonrecognition," and reserved the right, throughout the Kennedy presidency, to take "appropriate action" against Mao's China. Lyndon Johnson was dispatched to Taipei to ease Chiang's mind, but the Nationalist leader's "appropriate action" decision remained firm. *Time* magazine's special

1961 issue on Chinese affairs did not help matters either. America's favorite weekly news journal denounced nonrecognition as "foolish policy for the 1960s," and urged a reassessment of ROC–U.S. relations.[68]

Could the New Pacific Community, if ever welcomed by the Asian/ Pacific nations, manage Kennedy's China dilemma? Lyndon Johnson thought the organization was more an expression of New Frontier idealism than a workable policy. He had told Chiang that the United States would not tolerate any military action in the Taiwan Strait, and that the new international organization hoped to isolate Mao even more. On the other hand, he told Kennedy that it would be difficult to keep Chiang "leashed," and it would be even more difficult to build the New Pacific Community. Johnson called his observations "realistic." Robert Kennedy wondered if the crusty wheel-and-deal Johnson could ever be a "real" New Frontiersman.[69]

China policy remained hitched to the fate of the New Pacific Community plan. Meanwhile, border tensions between India and China during the middle of Kennedy's presidency would bring press and congressional focus on the White House's China endeavors. As in the case of the other three major "dilemmas," Kennedy wished the China issue could somehow resolve itself. India's sword rattling over border matters added to Kennedy's frustrations.

Despite glowing public speeches on behalf of Indian democracy, the Kennedy administration privately had serious misgivings over Indian power. In the tradition of raw anticommunism and nonrecognition of Chinese extremism, the issues contributing to Chinese-Indian tensions were irrelevant. Publicly, China was denounced for harassing India, and the reasons for the row were not discussed. The State Department reacted similarly when discussing Chinese-Indian relations with Congress; in confidence, however, Rusk did admit to several senators that the Kennedy administration saw no heroes in the disagreement between China and India.[70] The Kennedy team had spent many hours discussing India's regrettable attraction to nonalignment; the influence of Khrishna Menon, the charismatic Indian defense minister, on the growth of pro-Soviet political sentiment in India; the Indian government's reluctance to consider disarmament as an important option for peace; and the impact of radical politics upon the Indian military. All these matters obviously troubled the Kennedy team, and the contrast with official statements surprised the Senate Armed Services Committee.

Senator Symington wondered if a possible American mediation of disputes between "two unlikables" (China and India) in American policy might lead to direct U.S. recognition of China. Rusk later explained to Symington and his Armed Services colleagues that it would take more than one issue to stimulate U.S. recognition of China. It would have to involve a Chinese commitment to peace throughout Southeast Asia, a Chinese denunciation of aggression, and "a firm community of American alliances with friendly powers" to ensure that China kept its word. Rusk insisted that all this was possible, but probably not until after July 1964, or another two years of Kennedy government.[71] He gave no reason for this target date, and Congress did not question Rusk's timetable.

Rusk's comments suggested that in 1962 Kennedy idealism over the "firm community of alliances" (the New Pacific Community) had not waned. Moreover, the implication that within two years China would accept its fate as an outmanuevered government in Asia and welcome America's victorious overtures toward recognition gave a specific, optimistic twist to this tale. Even serious difficulties, such as the ultimate outbreak of hostilities between India and China, did not derail this optimism.

The trials of practical policy making and the range of foreign affairs crises dampened New Frontier enthusiasm by late 1963, but the desire to triumph over Chinese influence in Asia still burnt strong. Shortly before his assassination, Kennedy continued to speak in cabinet meetings about the necessity of Chinese isolation. He explained to Rusk that even if 110 nations signed his Nuclear Test Ban Treaty, China's refusal to sign it would be an American victory. The task of isolating China would be made easier if it refused to sign.[72] Peking obliged Kennedy here; however, effective tactics to isolate China did not emerge from this.

With the New Pacific Community plan in shambles by the end of his presidency, Kennedy turned more and more to bluffs, threats, and gamesmanship in Chinese affairs. He used intermediaries in Warsaw to suggest to China that an informal agreement, which the veteran diplomat W. Averell Harriman had just concluded with Chiang, was more militant than was actually the case. This agreement simply confirmed American opposition to Chiang's latest threats against the mainland, but provided that America would continue to protect the ROC as long as it maintained a "defensive posture." In an attempt to bluff the Chinese into believing that Harriman's trips had been a gesture in support of Chiang's saber rattling, the "defensive posture" clause was omitted from the 1963 Warsaw communications with China. The Chinese gave no official clue whether or not they were taken in by this bluff, but the international press had already speculated that Harriman's visit to Chiang had been designed to calm him down, not to encourage him.[73]

Hours before his ill-fated November 1963 trip to Dallas, the president mentioned to his attorney general brother that "China outmaneuvering" must play a major role in his "speech offensive" during the upcoming swing tour of Asia and Micronesia. He planned a three-day stopover in Hong Kong, hoping to offer a dramatic "Ich bin ein Berliner"-styled speech there. The anti-China effort required a little drama, he said. Robert Kennedy reminded his brother that dramatic rhetoric had had little impact on the Berlin situation. Quoting the president's favorite remark when he was confused and frustrated over a given policy, the attorney general commented wryly to his brother that the presidency might soon be showing "more profile than courage" over the China issue.[74] Nevertheless, as always, time was declared on their side. They would work it out after the Dallas trip. Maybe.

The Kennedy team had had nearly one elected term of office to work through a China policy and solve the other three privately proclaimed "dilemmas." On November 22, 1963, they ran out of time. The Kennedy White House had assumed the 1960s was their decade. Pesky problems would be solved eventually, and the American people educated to accept new paths in foreign affairs. Yet, Kennedy could never embark on that path himself if dilemmas obstructing it were ignored or avoided. Solving old cold war problems in a new fashion, or solving them at all, was labeled dangerous. The New Frontier's appeal of youthful innovation required action before the electorate derided the Kennedy team as "just another bunch of politicians." Dallas spared them this painful irony.

ENDNOTES

1. "Idealism's Rebirth," *U.S. News and World Report*, Vol. 105, No. 16 (October 24, 1988), p. 38.
2. "Taking the Long View in Foreign Affairs" (Kennedy Cabinet Briefing

Paper), October 8, 1963, Box 34 of the Theodore Sorensen Papers, JFK Library.

3. "Briefing on the Berlin Situation," *Executive Sessions of the Senate Foreign Relations Committee, 1961* Vol. XIII, Part 2 (Washington, D.C., 1985), p. 189; Eugene Brown, *J. William Fulbright: Advice and Dissent* (Iowa City; 1985), p. 1.

4. "NSC Record of Actions-Africa," November 7, 1961, Box 52 of the Theodore Sorensen Papers, JFK Library.

5. Warren I. Cohen, *Dean Rusk* (Totowa, N.J., 1980), pp. 128–129.

6. Although the author often describes the inner feelings of the participants without adequate footnoting, the following work remains a fine, detailed account of Berlin events (January 1961–mid-August 1961). Honoré M. Catudal, *Kennedy and the Berlin Wall Crisis: A Case Study in U.S. Decision Making* (Berlin, 1980). See also: Robert Slusser, *The Berlin Crisis of 1961* (Baltimore, MD, 1973).

7. "National Security Action Memorandum No. 62–Berlin," July 24, 1961, NSF/Box 330, JFK Library.

8. *Ibid.*; Parmet, *JFK*, p. 190; Burner, *John F. Kennedy*, pp. 72–75.

9. Classified Subject Files: Berlin, July 1961, Box 52 of the Theodore Sorensen Papers, JFK Library.

10. Schlesinger, *Thousand Days*, p. 391.

11. Kennedy to Schlesinger (on Goldwater and Berlin), December 4, 1961, WH-11 of the Arthur Schlesinger Papers, JFK Library.

12. "Report of the Military Assistance Steering Groups," December 12, 1961, Box 52 of the Theodore Sorensen Papers, JFK Library. Henry Trewhitt, *McNamara* (New York, 1971), p. 18.

13. Kaufmann, *McNamara Strategy*, p. 40; Desmond Ball, *Politics and Force Levels: The Strategic Missile Program of the Kennedy Administration* (Berkeley, CA, 1980), p. 190.

14. The French even worried about a combined U.S.–German conspiracy against their interests in Europe. See: Manfred Jonas, *The United States and Germany: A Diplomatic History* (Ithaca, 1984), p. 285. "Basic National Security Policy," February 27, 1962, POF/Box 88, JFK Library.

15. "Basic National Security Policy," March 25, 1963, and NSC Papers: France and United Kingdom, April 2, 1963, NSF/Box 294 and Box 52 of the Theodore Sorensen Papers, JFK Library.

16. Kennedy to Western European Heads-of-State, January 24, 1963, POF/Box 42, JFK Library.

17. See Chapter 6 of this work.

18. "Foreign Affairs Policy Briefing Conference–Africa," August 15, 1961, Box 34 of the Theodore Sorensen Papers, JFK Library.

19. *Ibid.* For Ball and his visions of a New Frontier for Africa, see: George Ball, *The Past Has Another Pattern* (New York, 1982), pp. 226–234.

20. Ambassador James Gavin (France) to Rusk, September 21, 1961, NSF/Box 4, JFK Library.

21. Ball, *Past*, pp. 226–234.

22. Thomas Noer, *Cold War and Black Liberation: The United States and White Rule in Africa, 1948–1968* (Columbia, MO, 1985), p. 60. G. Mennen Williams, *Africa for Africans* (Grand Rapids, Mich., 1969), p. 172. Williams was Kennedy's assistant secretary of State for African Affairs.

23. "Briefing on the Congo Situation," Rusk testimony to Senate Foreign Relations and Armed Services committees, January 18, 1962, *Executive Sessions*, Vol. XIV, pp. 111–133.

24. *Ibid.*, pp. 111–141; Rusk to Kennedy, August 3, 1961, NSF/Box 28, JFK Library. Richard Mahoney, *JFK: Ordeal in Africa* (New York, 1983), pp. 38–40.

25. Ball, *Past*, pp. 226–234. "Mission to Africa" report, Bowles to Kennedy, February 1962, NSF/Box 3, JFK Library. "Changing Situation in the Congo," Rusk statement to Senate Foreign Relations and Armed Services Committees, January 11, 1963, *Executive Sessions*, Vol. XU, pp. 33–35.

26. Briefing Papers and Transcript of the Kennedy-Mikoyan meeting, November 29, 1962, Box 49 of the Sorensen Papers, JFK Library. Much of the Kennedy-Mikoyan meeting was kept secret until early 1992. A 1992 conference in Havana, consisting of the surviving diplomatic sparring partners of the Cuban Bay of Pigs and Missile crises, helped to stimulate declassifications. See: "McNamara faults Cuba for tensions with U.S." *Boston Globe*, January 10, 1992, p. 2.

27. Sorensen, *Kennedy*, p. 454; Heller to Kennedy, November 28, 1961, Box 29 of the Theodore Sorensen Papers, JFK Library.

28. "Proposals for 1962 United States Foreign Trade and Tariff Legislation," October 4, 1961, POF/Box 50, JFK Library. Thomas Zeiler, "Free Trade Politics and Diplomacy," *Diplomatic History*, Vol. XI (Spring 1987), pp. 127–142.

29. Ball to Kennedy and follow-up report on the October 4, 1961 "Proposals for 1962 United States Foreign Trade and Tariff Legislation," October 23, 1961, POF/Box 50.

30. *Ibid.*

31. *Ibid.*; Kennedy to Congress: "Special Message on Trade," January 24, 1962, POF/Box 50, JFK library; Robert Pastor, *Congress and the Politics of U.S. Foreign Economic Policy, 1929–1976* (Berkeley, 1980), p. 70.

32. Rusk to Kennedy and "Review of Export Control Policy," and "United States Economic Defense Policy," July 10, 1962, Box 52 of the Theodore Sorensen Papers, JFK Library. Executive privilege is stressed more than economic principle in this correspondence and analysis.

33. *Ibid.*; Ball, *The Past*, pp. 188–198. Ball to Kennedy, October 23, 1961, POF/Box 50, JFK Library.

34. Kennedy-Mikoyan meeting transcripts, November 29, 1962, Box 49 of the Theodore Sorensen Papers, JFK Library.

35. Rusk to Kennedy, November 29, 1962, ibid.

36. *Congressional Quarterly Almanac, 1963* (Washington, D.C., 1964), pp. 264–265; Sorensen to Kennedy and "National Trade Policy" memo, January 8, 1962, POF/Box 50.

37. "U.S. Policy Problems Arising from Japanese Trade" a report of the subcommittee on Foreign Economic Policy, plus commentary by Arthur Schlesinger to Kennedy, November 20, 1961, WH-12a of Arthur Schlesinger Papers, JFK Library.
38. *Ibid.*; Briefing Material: Visit of Prime Minister Ikeda, State Department to Kennedy, June 23, 1961, JFK Library, POF/Box 120.
39. R. K. Jain, *China and Japan, 1949–76* (Atlantic Highlands, NJ, 1977), pp. 67–68; U.S. and U.S.S.R. trade relations during the Ikeda years is a major focus of Chitoshi Yanaga, *Big Business in Japanese Politics* (New Haven, 1968).
40. Edwin O. Reischauer, "An Overview," in Priscilla Clapp and Morton Halperin, eds., *United States–Japanese Relations: The 1970s* (Cambridge, MA, 1974), pp. 1–18.
41. O'Brien bill, May 4, 1961, White House Central Files/Box 62, JFK Library.
42. "Observations on Proposal for a New Pacific Community and Review of April Cabinet Session," November 2, 1961, NSF/Box 345, JFK Library.
43. Lawrence F. O'Brien, special assistant to the president, to Rep. John Baldwin, March 8, 1961, White House Central Files/Box 62.
44. *Ibid.*
45. Lawrence F. O'Brien to Rep. Leo O'Brien, and Bill O'Brien, May 4, 1961, *ibid.*
46. *Ibid.*
47. Minutes of Kennedy-Ikeda discussion, June 20–21, 1961 and Kennedy-Ikeda, "Joint Communique," June 22, 1961; Kennedy to Henry Luce, *Time/Life*, July 10, 1961; Memorandum and Report for Frederick P. Dutton, White House: "The United States–Japan Committee," October 12, 1961, POF/Box 120 and White House Central Files/Box 62, JFK Library. Reischauer, "The Broken Dialogue with Japan," *Foreign Affairs*, Vol. 39, (October 1960), pp. 11–16.
48. McGovern to Sen. Wayne Morse, October 13, 1961, White House Central Files/Box 62, JFK Library.
49. Hauge to the White House and Report on Trade Delegation Meetings, October 1961–February 1962, February 27, 1962, *ibid.*
50. "Proclamation Giving Effect to Trade Agreement Negotiations with Japan," February 1, 1963, POF/Box 120, JFK Library.
51. Ikeda to Kennedy, July 31, 1963, and Kennedy to the United States–Japan Conference on Cultural and Educational Interchange, October 15, 1963, White House Central Files/Box 62, JFK Library.
52. Minutes of the Kennedy-Ikeda discussion, June 20–21, 1961, POF/Box 120, JFK Library.
53. Timothy P. Maga, " 'Pay Any Price, Bear Any Burden': John F. Kennedy and Sino-American Relations, 1961–1963" in Priscilla Roberts, ed., *Sino-American Relations Since 1900* (Hong Kong, 1991), pp. 468–481; James Fetzer, "Clinging to Containment," *Kennedy's Quest for Victory*, pp. 178–197; James C. Thomson, Jr., "On the Making of U.S.–China Policy, 1961–1969: A Study in Bureaucratic Politics," *China Quarterly*, Vol. 50 (April–June 1972), pp. 221–222.

54. State Department Report: "China Policy and Contingency Planning for Possible Reviewed Chinese Communist Attack on the Offshore Islands," July 10, 1961, State Department Files/Box 141, JFK Library.
55. Briefing Material: Prime Minister Menzies Visit—China Discussions, February 22–24, 1961, POF/Box 111, JFK Library.
56. J. Wilcynski, "Australia's Trade with China," *India Quarterly* (April–June 1965), pp. 154–167. Gabriel Kolko *Anatomy of a War: Vietnam, The United States, and the Modern Historical Experience* (New York, 1985), p. 112. D. W. Rawson, "Foreign Policy and Australian Parties," *World Review* (July 1962), pp. 16–23. U.S.-Australian Relations: Australia's Internal Political Situation, State Department memo to Kennedy, March 13, 1962, POF/Box 111, JFK Library.
57. Kennedy-Menzies discussions: China, February 22–24, 1961, *ibid.*
58. Chiaing to Kennedy and Rusk comments concerning this communication, July 28, 1961, State Department Files/Box 141, JFK Library. Leonard H. D. Gordon, "United States Opposition to the Use of Force in the Taiwan Strait, 1954–1962," *The Journal of American History*, Vol. 72, No. 3, (December 1985), pp. 637–660.
59. "Contingency Planning. . . . ," June 23, 1961, State Department Files/Box 141, JFK Library.
60. Chiang to Kennedy and Rusk comments concerning this communication, July 28, 1961, *ibid.*
61. Briefing Material to Kennedy-Menzies discussions, February 22–24, 1961, POF/Box 111, JFK Library.
62. Kennedy-Menzies discussions: China, February 22–24, 1961, *ibid.*
63. *Ibid.*
64. "Briefing on U.S.-Communist China Relations," Rusk closed session report, *Executive Sessions of the Senate Foreign Relations Committee . . .* , 1961, Vol. XIII, March 1961 section.
65. *Ibid.*
66. *Ibid.*
67. Memorandum on Proposal for a New Pacific Community, November 2, 1961, NSF/Box 345, JFK Library.
68. NSC Assessment Report: "The Vice President's Visit to the Republic of China," May 16, 1961; Chiang to Kennedy, July 28, 1961; Kennedy to Luce, July 10, 1961, NSF/Box 345, State Department Files/Box 141, White House Central Files/Box 50, JFK Library.
69. "The Vice President's Visit. . . . ," May 16, 1961, NSF/Box 345, JFK Library.
70. Srinivas M. Chary, "Kennedy and Non-alignment: An Analysis of Indo-American Relations," Harper and Krieg, eds., *John F. Kennedy*, pp. 119–130. "The Situation in India, Testimony of Secretary Rusk and John Kenneth Galbraith, United States Ambassador to India," June 6–21, 1962, *Executive Sessions of the Senate Foreign Relations Committee. . . . 1962*, Vol. XIV, pp. 507–550.
71. *Ibid.* (last entry).
72. Testimony of Dean Rusk on Nuclear Test Ban Treaty, August 28–Septem-

ber 25, 1963, *Executive Sessions of the Senate Foreign Relations Committee. . . . 1963*, Vol. XV, pp. 423–638. Gordon Chang, "JFK, China, and the Bomb," *Journal of American History*, Vol. 74 (March 1988), pp. 1287–1310.
73. The Editors of *Congressional Quarterly, China-U.S. Policy Since 1945* (Washington, 1980), pp. 130–131.
74. NSC Report and Robert Kennedy comments: "China and East-West Tensions," November 1963, NSC report declassified for author, 1989.

CHAPTER 6

Foreign Policy at Home:
The Trials of the Special Protocol Service

Although he possessed no crystal ball, Kennedy foresaw the rise of the Third World in the 1960s. He even worried that a negative opinion of America in the minds of diplomats from newly decolonized nations could cost America a victory over the attractions of communism throughout the Third World.[1] Those worries, of course, were attached to the growing "Ugly American" image of U.S. representatives abroad. Hence, given the alleged arrogance and abrasiveness of American diplomats in developing countries, Washington appeared destined to defeat in the effort to win the allegiance of Third World residents trapped in the cold war.

Finally, after years of apparent shame and embarrassment, the tale of America's 1960s endeavor to win Third World "hearts and minds" had become the topic of numerous scholarly and popular writers. An important part of the early tale is often ignored, however. One of the major architects of the "hearts and minds" approach, John Kennedy, saw it as a two front war with foreign and domestic theaters. Erasing the "Ugly American" image abroad would never be good enough, he told the State Department in January 1961.[2] Every effort was required at home, he insisted, to convince the growing crowd of Third World diplomats in Washington that America renounced domestic racism, embraced full commitments to civil rights/civil liberties, and generally practiced at home the democratic faith that it preached abroad. Especially concerned about the number of incoming black African diplomats,

Kennedy believed that a State Department seminar or two for them on American life would not prepare them for the reality of American racial tension. Indeed, it would be an insult to their political intelligence. His answer to the Africans and to the domestic phase of anti-"Ugly American" diplomacy was the creation of the Special Protocol Service Section of the State Department.[3]

As part of Kennedy's so-called foreign policy "brain trust" at the end of the 1960 campaign, veteran diplomat and Democratic party activist Chester Bowles recommended the creation of the Special Protocol Service. Its establishment, he believed, would not compromise the foreign policy-making work of the State Department and, in most cases, it would not interfere in the work of federal, state, and local authorities at home. Stressing full civil rights/liberties protection for all Third World diplomats and their families in the nation's Capitol and across America, Bowles particularly worried about the impact of lingering Jim Crow laws and racist business practices when applied against black Africans. With predictions of nearly forty new nations emerging during Kennedy's "first term," Bowles feared that the United States might be its own worst enemy in the battle to win "hearts and minds." "The incidents involving African and other diplomats in which they have been refused service in public places are not only morally wrong," he told Kennedy, "but have most unfortunate repercussions abroad."[4]

Kennedy had no objection to an innovative idea. Bowles's call for a Special Protocol Service had been a specific plank within his larger plan for a top-to-bottom review of State Department personnel policy. The full plan was offered to Kennedy when Bowles was the designated undersecretary of state, and his boss, Dean Rusk, agreed. According to Bowles, the State Department's most competent personnel had been either hounded from their jobs during the early 1950s Red scare days of Senator Joe McCarthy, or they had fled to nongovernment positions that did not inflict them with Red-baiting troubles. The remainder, Bowles concluded, were rightists, racists, and abandoned Eisenhower sycophants. Their very existence on the payroll, he noted, had the potential of sabotaging Kennedy's New Frontier. Outside of firing the lot, deemed an impractical approach by Kennedy, new State Department sections, committed to the New Frontier vision of winning the cold War, made better bureaucratic sense.[5] The Special Protocol Service, therefore, was seen as part of this march to victory in the cold war.

Bowles's great reform of the State Department's staffing procedures failed as Kennedy turned to the arch cold warriors for advice. Cold war tensions obviously increased during the Berlin, Laos, and Cuban crises. Shifting and altering the foreign service bureaucracy, Kennedy reasoned, would send a signal of confusion and weakness to Moscow.[6] The Special Protocol Service Section, on the other hand, began its work in February 1961.

Kennedy's interest in the service idea was rooted in his own 1960 campaign rhetoric and in his fascination with the thesis, of course, of *The Ugly American*. Lederer and Burdick's message to American diplomats to find "the right key" abroad and "maneuver" whole Third World nations for American self-interest, anticommunism, and local development made great sense to Kennedy. "We must return," he proclaimed, "to the generous spirit; stress our positive interest in and moral responsibility for relieving misery and poverty; and acknowledge to ourselves and to the world that communism or no communism, we cannot be an island unto ourselves."[7] Bowles's call for a Special Protocol Service had received the new president's welcome attentions.[8] American–Third World relations could not continue on the assumption that "more military and economic aid would buy us friends," Kennedy reminded the State Department in January 1961. If Third World residents "feel that they are being made pawns in the Cold War, if they regard the United States only as a military guardian, a giver of goods or a lender of cash, then no amount of aid will strengthen our cause in that area."[9]

January and February 1961 were soon considered the "innocent days" of the New Frontier, according to historian and Kennedy aide Arthur Schlesinger, Jr. It was in this atmosphere of "innocent" euphoria that Kennedy concluded America must somehow resolve, or at least attempt to resolve, social tensions in the face of onrushing Third World diplomats. There was even a sense of urgency to the new work of the Special Protocol Service, for Dr. William Fitzjohn, the freshly arrived ambassador from Sierra Leone, had been denied service at several Washington, D.C.-area restaurants and refused housing in the neighborhoods of his choice. Outraged, Fitzjohn urged the breaking of U.S.–Sierra Leone relations. His anger was calmed by the Sierra Leone government; however, the prime minister of Sierra Leone fired off a markedly unpleasant greeting to the new American president. "If conditions in the

U.S. are typified by the recent news involving Dr. Fitzjohn, I do not care to lead the Sierra Leone delegation to the U.N. General Assembly in New York."[10]

At the same time as the Fitzjohn matter, the new second secretary of the Nigerian Embassy was refused breakfast in a Washington, D.C., restaurant, given some food in a paper bag, and told, under threats of violence, to eat it elsewhere "with other niggers." The Nigerian government assailed the Kennedy administration, noting that it entertained the recall of its ambassador. "By this disgraceful act of racial discrimination, the U.S. forfeits its claim to world leadership," the Nigerian government declared.[11]

The Special Protocol Service had its work cut out. Technically, Kennedy was its chief and the overall administrator of protocol matters was Angier Biddle Duke. Yet, in reality, the working director of this "Special" agency was Pedro Sanjuan. A Hispanic-American Democratic party activist, Sanjuan had been brought to Kennedy's attention due to his efforts to elevate civil rights/liberties for residents of the American territories from Puerto Rico to Guam. A strong believer in the promise of the New Frontier, Sanjuan adored Kennedy and also regarded him as a close friend.[12] The feelings would not be mutual, largely because Sanjuan soon took his antiracism mission more seriously than Kennedy.

Whereas Kennedy spoke broadly of a new America that would welcome Third World diplomats and not harass them, Sanjuan was required to work with a limited budget trickled through the undersecretary of state's office. Somehow, he was expected to keep arriving diplomats from quickly returning home. The Sierra Leone and Nigeria episodes provided a key to specific means of success. Sanjuan offered tearful apologies for these matters, urging African patience in anticipation of great reforms to come. The apologies were not accepted. Nigeria, for instance, considered the second secretary matter "an insult to the entire country."[13] In any event, Sanjuan hoped someday to address Congress, then the "mayor" of Washington, D.C., as well as the nearby state legislatures of Maryland and Virginia. Racist codes and practices in the restaurant and real estate businesses would be assaulted in these locations, whereby he would ask for special consideration before the law in the cases of Third World diplomats.

The politics of special consideration, on the other hand, was difficult and Sanjuan knew it would be. More to the point, Sanjuan preferred to destroy all Jim Crow laws related to food and housing in the Washington, D.C., area. He anticipated Kennedy's support in this endeavor, but he would always be placing the president in a precarious position over jurisdiction and priorities.[14] The State Department was an odd and unlikely vehicle to lead an antiracist crusade on home turf. Congressmen as well as Maryland and Virginia state legislators reminded Sanjuan of that reality. Furthermore, it was extremely difficult to create special civil rights protection for what amounted to foreign blacks versus the majority of black American citizens in Washington, D.C. Sanjuan was reminded of that point as well. Finally, Sanjuan stressed that successful anticommunist endeavors in the Third World hinged upon how domestic legislators responded to his call to action at home. This established a certain emergency agenda against racism that actually moved faster than Kennedy's own civil rights legislation in Congress.

Sanjuan was a mover and shaker; however, from the tactical point of view, he won the reputation of trying to move and shake too quickly.[15] Sanjuan's office polled as many eating establishments in the D.C. area as possible and canvassed the likely and usual housing/apartment choices of the diplomatic corps. By March 1961, their studies were complete, and with Kennedy's blessing, they urged that both incoming Third World diplomats and those already settled check in with the Special Protocol Service. While placing or relocating diplomats in "racially safe" residences and offering "hospitable" restaurant advice, Sanjuan promised prosecution of all those locales which did not fall in the "racially safe" and "hospitable" categories.[16]

Pursuing racists in the courts, and hoping that a judge would manufacture a sweeping decision in favor of desegregation, was not Sanjuan's style. Expecting faster results, he preferred the political arena to the courts. By mid-1961, he had won the support of thirty-eight governors, excluding those of Maryland and Virginia. That meant all thirty-eight had signed a Sanjuan-drafted document, establishing themselves as on-call advisors to Maryland and Virginia in the effort to eliminate Jim Crow laws. Sanjuan would referee the advising procedure. Despite the growing complaint from state legislators that America's foreign policy-making machinery was interfering in local politics and traditions, Sanjuan kept up the pressure.

Nearly all of the twenty-two Third World diplomats who arrived in America for the first time in the summer of 1961 were Africans. All of them had been contacted by Sanjuan before they left home. Both verbally and in writing, Sanjuan had informed them in a frank and detailed fashion about racially divided America. Hence, cultural shock was lessened, and, perhaps, the strength of Sierra Leone/Nigeria–styled complaints against America might also be lessened in consequence. Although, theoretically, the new Third World diplomats represented their nation's political "best and brightest," Sanjuan found them quite ignorant of American life and culture. At best, they had an idealist's view of Constitutional democracy or a certain textbook knowledge of basic American history. Consequently, Sanjuan saw himself as Third World educator and antiracist prosecutor. Both roles would also benefit the larger anti-"Ugly American" effort, and, Sanjuan hoped, please the president.[17]

"Response time" to racial incidents, and the proper response itself, was a matter of debate in the Special Protocol Service in its early months; however, a procedure was established and maintained by late 1961. During the fall of 1961, the new ambassador from Chad, enroute to the White House to present his credentials to Kennedy, was refused restaurant service on Route 40 in Maryland. Quite disturbed by the matter, the ambassador informed Kennedy that Sanjuan had warned him about such possibilities. Nevertheless, the timing of the incident, i.e., credentials presentation day, carried a certain symbolic significance to the ambassador. Hence, he never formally presented his credentials. He returned to Chad, recommending a more "tolerant" diplomat for the job.[18]

Taken aback by yet another incident, Kennedy ordered Sanjuan "to do something." The new "response" procedure was engaged. A lengthy and very formal apology was sent directly to the Chad government. An excellent forgery of the president's signature was affixed to the bottom of it. Sanjuan offered personal apologies to the Chad embassy. Meanwhile, he received support from the majority of the thirty-eight governors to condemn the state legislature of Maryland. That condemnation was accompanied by a "demand" to speak in front of a joint session of the Maryland legislature in order to address "this grave matter" in both foreign and domestic policy. Finally, he contacted Maryland's civil rights lobbyists and activist groups, stating that "the president wanted" them to picket restaurants across Route 40.

Sanjuan called his "response" procedure "The Wedge," for it positioned itself in the heart of the Jim Crow status quo. It was usually effective as well. Thirty-five of the seventy-five restaurants on Route 40, anticipating weeks of negative media publicity, slow business, and punitive legislation, voluntarily released their "white only" rules within days after the Chad incident. Despite the typical complaint against a State Department chief "speaking on internal problems," the Maryland legislature accepted Sanjuan's "demand." On September 13, 1961, he offered his usual impassioned speech against the "Ugly American" and in favor of equal rights. Stating that all he could do is ask them to support the State Department's interests, he reminded the legislature that winning the cold war was Maryland's business as well. The Route 40 episode, he said, hurt the chances of that victory. He urged them to support a public accommodations bill that would end all "white only" rules in Maryland housing, restaurants, and other establishments.

> The issue before the world today is whether democracy works better than tyranny or tyranny better than democracy. Your aid and support in passing the Public Accommodations Bill will eliminate a source of embarrassment that greatly damages our relations with not only the neutral nations of the world, but many nations which are stoutly with us in the fight for freedom. This Bill if passed will prove that democracy does work, that in a democracy the rights and privileges of the individual are protected in accordance with the will of the people. . . . The Department of State comes to you now with a request. GIVE US THE WEAPONS TO CONDUCT THIS WAR OF HUMAN DIGNITY. The fight for decency against Communism is everyone's war in America.[19]

The bill passed.

On October 25, 1961, E. M. Debrah, counselor of the Embassy of Ghana, addressed a UNESCO conference in Boston on the topic of racism in America and its impact on African opinion. Debrah, who had been a victim of housing discrimination, was expected to slander the American government, but, instead, he stunned some American observers with his praises for Sanjuan's office. Kennedy's New Frontier was, as his inaugural address had promised, "taking the first step" in the battle against racism. Depending on the success of Kennedy's pending civil rights legislation and the continuing commitment of the Special Protocol Service, Debrah predicted a healthy U.S.–Third World relationship in the 1960s. His tone was cautious, but, in general, Debrah's speech was welcome news to the Kennedy team. Lloyd Garrison, who covered the speech for *The New York Times* and was considered the paper's Third World expert, claimed that American victory over communist attractions in Africa and even elsewhere was "now in reach."

Debrah's address had been applauded by the Third World participants at the conference, and Garrison was always surprised at "the lack of hostility" toward the United States. That surprise apparently influenced his upbeat assessment on Kennedy's approaching victories across the Third World. If anything, the more accommodating opinion toward America at the United Nations Educational, Scientific, and Cultural Organization (UNESCO) conference represented an African-led thank you for Sanjuan's work and best wishes for continued success in the long struggles ahead. Debrah and his colleagues had said nothing about Kennedy's cold war victory dreams and probably had little interest in them.[20]

Thanks to the positive press and African diplomatic corps approval, Sanjuan moved on to bolder measures. New procedures were enacted. First of all, U.S. embassies in the African Third World were asked to survey their host governments' diplomats with an elaborate survey form. The form polled their views on racial discrimination, expectations of American reform politics, ideas on housing and travel assistance from the Special Protocol Service, and the issues of American life and culture that frustrated them. The poll was widely distributed and the responses reflected deep-rooted fears of an American assignment. Kennedy worried that the survey might trouble the everyday work of these diplomats, but he had done nothing to halt it.

Second, Sanjuan began a letter-writing campaign to realtor and restaurant associations, suggesting that the president would be upset if racist practices in their ranks continued. Sanjuan was careful to stress the diplomatic importance of his request, but, again, Kennedy worried that Sanjuan's new boldness was becoming too intimidating and too rooted in his own attractions to domestic civil rights causes. The charge was a sad one, for Sanjuan believed he was following through New Frontier commitments and enjoyed the president's trust. Nevertheless, Kennedy remained aloof from the emotion of civil rights crusading, even though he had a strong intellectual appreciation for its necessity.[21]

Third, Sanjuan was concerned that his new agency did not enjoy much visibility in the federal government bureaucracy. With the active support of other agencies, from the Civil Rights Commission to the Federal Bureau of Investigation, his message of antiracist protection for diplomats might be more effective. He proposed personal addresses to hordes of bureaucrats, hoping that his fiery speaking style would bring him the required visibility as well as converts to his cause. In his addresses, he suggested forming liaison offices with most of the federal agencies. The diplomatic and emergency characteristics of his work demanded a broadening of his office's influence within government, or so he believed.[22]

By 1962, the Kennedy cabinet was discussing the possibility of replacing Sanjuan with a less crusading personality. An individual more concerned about the cold war aspects of his mission rather than its civil rights proportions was preferable. Walt Rostow, former Massachusetts Institute of Technology professor, Kennedy national security advisor, and reliable cold warrior, was recommended by Kennedy aides McGeorge Bundy and Carl Keysen. William Battle, former PT-boat colleague of Kennedy and son of the governor of Virginia, was seen as an adequate alternative to Rostow. As a good Virginia Democrat, Battle could ease the tensions that Sanjuan had caused there and before the 1962 congressional elections. Yet, Kennedy, upon the impassioned advice of Arthur Schlesinger, decided to keep Sanjuan for a little while longer.[23] Rostow did not want the job anyway, and Battle preferred an ambassadorial post in the Pacific. The latter won an appointment to Australia.

Sanjuan, for the time being, was secure. He had no idea the White House viewed him as a civil rights extremist who remained only moderately concerned over cold war victory. For all effective purposes, Sanjuan had juggled his civil rights and anti-"Ugly American" priorities quite well and won results. The White House, troubled by foreign policy crises and growing civil rights tensions in the South, forgot the idealism of early 1961.[24] Sanjuan still embraced it and remained entranced by Kennedy's glowing rhetoric and promise. He never viewed his pace as too fast or too politically treacherous for the Democratic party.[25]

During the spring of 1962, Kennedy discovered that racial tensions with diplomatic connections were not necessarily centered in D.C. or surrounding Southern states. Chukyuma Azikiwe, a Nigerian student at Harvard and the son of the governor general of Nigeria, was arrested for rape by Cambridge, Massachusetts, police. Beaten and insulted by the arresting officers, Azikiwe considered confessing to the crime but continually claimed his innocence. He spent one night in a holding cell where he was brutalized by its inmates as well. Azikiwe's Harvard house master rescued him, and the police later admitted they had incarcerated the wrong man. The young Nigerian preferred to forget the matter. His father did not.

The elder Azikiwe sought a formal apology from the Kennedy administration and intended to sue the city of Cambridge for millions of dollars. Meanwhile, he favored a special summit with Kennedy to discuss the sorry state of U.S.-Nigerian relations, implying that repair to that relationship remained elusive. Adding to these troubles, the mayor of Cambridge announced that he would not permit his city to be financially straightjacketed by a foreign government. Although shocked by the incident at his alma mater, Kennedy was not interested in answering Azikiwe and hoped Sanjuan could remedy the situation.

Sanjuan sent an aide to Cambridge city hall, urging the city government to draft a tearful apology to Azikiwe or face undefined "actions" against them from their "favorite son" in the White House, Kennedy. Sanjuan worked on Governor General Azikiwe, reminding him that his son sought no revenge. By July 1962, the crisis had disappeared. The Cambridge city hall apologized and even the chief of police, in a special public ceremony, offered his regrets to young Azikiwe.[26]

The Azikiwe matter was the most dramatic of the racial diplomatic incidents during the first half of 1962; however, there were complaints of racial disturbance issued by the embassies of Kuwait, Dahomey, Jamaica, Syria, and Morocco. Two embassies, Sudan and Turkey, praised the Special Protocol Service for its assistance during this same period, and Sanjuan told Kennedy that more positive responses should be expected now. The worst was over, he said.[27] Indeed, these predictions, coupled to his decent handling of the Azikiwe matter, kept Sanjuan's post alive.

By late 1962, Sanjuan's lobbying of state officials had truly succeeded. Headed by Governor John H. Reed of Maine, a state liaison office was formally established, including representatives from forty-five states and two territories. Its most active member was Governor Terry Sanford of North Carolina who called D.C.-based Third World diplomats to meet various business and civic leaders in his state for a special antiracism convention. Meanwhile, he chided other state liaison members for not doing enough, and he urged Kennedy to grant special sweeping power to Sanjuan's office.[28] Kennedy never answered the request.

Sanjuan's image in the White House as the overly zealous bureaucrat lived on. During 1962, the vice-chancellor of the University College of the West Indies was arrested by immigration and customs authorities on smuggling charges. After a slow-moving investigation that ignored the vice-chancellor's pleas of innocence, the Justice Department admitted they had arrested the wrong man. Their real suspect had the same name and a similar appearance, but he had managed to escape. Sanjuan's resulting charges of incompetence against the Immigration and Naturalization Service were loud and angry. Disturbed by the ungentlemanly behavior and by insults to fellow New Frontiersmen, Kennedy began to number Sanjuan's days once again.[29]

Assuming that his biggest problem involved a misunderstanding of his mission by Kennedy aides and longtime foreign policy-makers, Sanjuan proposed special briefings for them. He now had a catchy term for his diplomatic/racial protection work, "statesidemanship." With supportive diplomats from African embassies in tow, Sanjuan dispatched his top aides on briefing missions to the Kennedy cabinet and State Department offices. If his personality was too unacceptable to the Kennedy team, he would at least provide an adequate defense of his endeavors through the briefings of his associates.[30]

Once again, Sanjuan won the opportunity to maintain his mission. The "statesidemanship" briefings were successful, and one of the New Frontiersmen most impressed with this effort was the president's brother, Attorney General Robert Kennedy. Attorney General Kennedy had taken no interest in the Special Protocol Service previously, but its record of civil rights success now added a supportive foundation to his own civil rights legislation.

In an effort to gain more visibility for his office and for Robert Kennedy's interests, Sanjuan proposed expensive bimonthly "Orientation United States" gatherings of Third World diplomats and American officials. In elegant surroundings, the participants would enjoy gourmet American food, listen to live traditional and popular American music, and be wooed by glowing speeches from Kennedy White House officials. The attorney general would be master of ceremonies for each function. From January to April 1963, the orientation gatherings, usually held at the State Department's West Auditorium, were standing-room-only successes. Several guests often had to sit in the aisles or stand in the back of the dining area. Robert Kennedy associated his civil rights interests with Sanjuan's in his speeches, making the latter feel more secure in his position and offering excellent propaganda opportunities for both men.[31]

Despite the Attorney General's newly found interest in the Special Protocol Service, Sanjuan was always on his own when dealing with Third World VIP's who had, in fact, committed crimes. The case of

Farag Bel Kassem Misallati in 1963 provided special problems. A Libyan student at Berkeley and the son of a wealthy politician, Farag passed thousands of dollars worth of bad checks during the first semester of his studies. During a visit to Reno, Nevada, he engaged in the same procedure, and local authorities even included him within a counterfeiting investigation. Upon Farag's arrest, the Libyan embassy claimed that their citizen was a victim of American racism. An apology from Kennedy was demanded. The district attorneys for both Berkeley and Reno requested Farag's deportation and petitioned the Libyan embassy for economic restitution. Meanwhile, Farag would be held in a Berkeley jail until deportation was arranged and restitution made. The Special Protocol Service informed the Libyans that the racism charge was unsubstantiated. No White House apology would be forthcoming; however, a "good faith" compromise was reached. Farag was released from his Berkeley confinement until full restitution and deportation arrangements were made.

Although the Libyans maintained their racism charges, accusing Sanjuan also of hypocrisy and conspiracy, the Special Protocol Service's decision remained final. Farag was deported and the Libyan embassy offered restitution in March 1963. A similar case in the same year involving M. Ata Rabbani, the air attaché of the Embassy of Pakistan, flared U.S.-Pakistan relations briefly, but deportation and restitution continued to remain the twin policies of the Special Protocol Service in the face of criminal activity. Rabbani had used his position to mask involvement in an elaborate car theft ring that brought dozens of cars and/or their components from the streets of Washington, D.C., to Pakistan.[32]

Criminal activities or not, the Third World embassies involved railed against American racism in the effort to protect their citizens. They also claimed special diplomatic privilege above the law; however, Sanjuan urged that these new embassies accept true diplomatic responsibilities and respect the laws of their host country. It was a paternalistic message, but criminal activities lessened throughout 1963. Moreover, the racism charges were often short-lived and, since Kennedy chose to ignore them in these cases, they never enjoyed the effect that the Third World embassies desired. Although sensitive to racism charges from any embassy, the Kennedy administration remained focused on institutionalized racism in America.

Sanjuan survived his post beyond the Kennedy assassination of November 1963. Nevertheless, he rarely saw the president in the last months of his life, for the pariah image continued.[33] Kennedy's civil rights promise remained more progressive than his record, and Sanjuan provided plenty of visibility for both that promise and the anti-"Ugly American" crusade. Yet, Sanjuan's commitment and tactics continued to trouble Kennedy, for they suggested a certain urgency that might, in the long run, injure his political career. Often, Kennedy spoke of taking the "first step" in relieving racial tension and winning the cold war.[34] Sanjuan sought solutions, not "first steps" toward them. The two Democrats worked with different agendas, but Sanjuan never wavered in his adulation of the young president. To Sanjuan, he was always America's best hope. The achievements of the Special Protocol Service would be Kennedy's achievements, and Sanjuan offered no apologies for this bureaucratic selflessness.

President Lyndon Johnson had little use for a Special Protocol Service. Like Sanjuan, he favored quicker solutions to major problems. Sanjuan, on the other hand, remained happier with the New Frontier than with the Great Society.[35] Moreover, Johnson never appreciated the complex and delicate tasks that had been accorded the Special Protocol Service. Sanjuan enjoyed balancing foreign and domestic policy priorities within the mandate of his duties. He always bemoaned the passing of his hero, John Kennedy.

The Special Protocol Service had been a classic New Frontier decision, reflecting the "can do" philosophy of the Kennedy team in 1961. It influenced the civil rights movement, but never served as solid foundation for civil rights legislation. It influenced U.S.-Third World relations, but never eradicated "Ugly Americanism" and never swayed Third World diplomats away from superpower doubt and suspicion. Instead, it defended certain diplomats from a racially divided society, worked to change that society, and provided a positive image of a concerned American government in the eyes of an often times confused diplomatic corps. The Special Protocol Service's influences and individual successes were accomplished, like so many of the positive changes in the 1960s, with some pain. Their endeavors merit recognition in both civil rights and cold war histories, as well as within the Camelot legacy.

ENDNOTES

1. "The United States and Our Future in Asia," Excerpts from the Remarks of Senator John F. Kennedy (Hawaii, 1958), JFK Library, Senate Files.

Stephen Wayne, *The Road to the White House: The Politics of Presidential Elections* (New York, 1984), Chapters 6–8.
2. "The Special Protocol Service Section, A Recent History," Acting Secretary of State Chester Bowles to Kennedy, September 20, 1961, JFK Library; Papers of Pedro Sanjuan, MS78-21/Campaign in Maryland.
3. *Ibid.*, "General Report on the First Nine Months," November 1, 1961; *ibid*/General Reports.
4. Bowles to Kennedy, September 19, 1961, and Department of State Press Release on the Special Protocol Service Section, *ibid*/Campaign in Maryland.
5. *Ibid.* Secretary of State Dean Rusk to Kennedy, February 2, 1961, JFK Library, POF/Box 111.
6. "General Report on the First Nine Months," November 1, 1961, JFK Library, Papers of Pedro Sanjuan, MS78-21/General Reports. Kennedy's early struggles as a foreign policy decision-maker have been well reviewed; however, one of the finest analyses of Kennedy's policy-making contradictions remains Kenneth W. Thompson, "Kennedy's Foreign Policy: Activism versus Pragmatism" in Paul Harper and Joann Krieg, *John F. Kennedy: The Promise Revisited* (New York, 1988), pp. 25–34.
7. William J. Lederer and Eugene Burdick, *The Ugly American* (New York, 1958), pp. 163, 233; Joseph Buttinger, "Fact and Fiction on Foreign Aid, A Critique of The Ugly American," *Dissent, A Quarterly of Socialist Opinion*, Vol. 6, Summer 1959, pp. 319–320. "The Ugly American Revisited," *Saturday Evening Post*, May 4, 1963, p. 78; Campaign Speech–Honolulu, JFK Library, 1960 Campaign/Hawaii.
8. James MacGregor Burns, *The Power to Lead* (New York, 1984), p. 75; Arthur M. Schlesinger, Jr., *The Cycles of American History* (Boston, 1986), p. 405.
9. Kennedy to Rusk, February 2, 1961 and Press Release: "Our Future in Asia," JFK Library, POF/Box 111.
10. Report No. 644: "The Fitzjohn Affair," Bowles to Kennedy, September 19, 1961, JFK Library, Papers of Pedro Sanjuan, MS78-21/Campaign in Maryland.
11. Study Report: "Living Conditions of New Diplomats in Washington and Vicinity and Suggestions for Easing of Tensions by the Office of Protocol," February 23, 1961, *ibid*/Living Conditions.
12. "General Observations," Sanjuan to Kennedy, February 23, 1961, *ibid.*
13. *Ibid.*
14. "Specific Problems," (Undated report, probably February–March 1961), Sanjuan to Kennedy, *ibid.*
15. Kennedy to John Field, the President's Committee for Equal Employment Opportunity, September 22, 1961, *ibid*/Campaign in Maryland.
16. "Self-Criticism and Foreign Policy," Address by Pedro Sanjuan to the national convention of the Civil Liberties Union, November 1, 1961, *ibid*/Speeches.
17. "General Report on the First Nine Months," November 1, 1961, *ibid*/General Reports.

18. Report on "The Chad Affairs," October 25, 1961, *ibid.*
19. *Ibid.*; Address by Sanjuan to the state legislature of Maryland, September 13, 1961, *ibid*/Campaign in Maryland.
20. General Report: "Tangible Effects of the Work of the Special Protocol Service Section on African Diplomats," November 1961 and report by the U.S. National Commission for UNESCO, "The Effect of the Existence of 'Segregation' in the U.S. on the American Image in Africa," October 25, 1961, *ibid*/General Reports and E. M. Debrah Files.
21. Progress Report, July 1, 1962; Memorandum for Mr. Bundy: "The President and the Special Protocol Service Section, with remarks by Mr. Schlesinger," December 8, 1961, JFK Library, Papers of Pedro Sanjuan, MS78-21/Progress Reports, and Papers of Arthur M. Schlesinger, WH-19/State Department. David Burner, *John F. Kennedy and a New Generation* (Glenview, Illinois, 1988), pp. 31–32, 158–159.
22. Progress Report, December 1, 1962, JFK Library, Papers of Pedro Sanjuan, MS78-21/Progress Reports.
23. Memorandum for Mr. Bundy: "The President and the Special Protocol Service Section, with remarks by Mr. Schlesinger," December 8, 1961, JFK Library, Papers of Arthur M. Schlesinger, WH-19/State Department.
24. For a review of Kennedy's priority politics and the place of practical foreign policy making within it, see: Thomas Paterson, ed., *Kennedy's Quest for Victory: American Foreign Policy, 1961–63* (New York, 1989), pp. 3–23.
25. Testimony of Pedro Sanjuan, "Public Hearing on the Question of Discrimination in Housing," Washington, D.C., December 1962, JFK Library, Papers of Pedro Sanjuan, MS78-21/Hearings.
26. "Incident Report: Chukyuma Azikiwe," July 1, 1962, *ibid*/Incidents.
27. Progress Report, December 1, 1962, *ibid*/Progress Reports.
28. *Ibid.*
29. Kennedy to Sanjuan, February 1, 1963, *ibid*/Correspondence.
30. "Orientation, U.S.A.—Progress Report," February 1963, *ibid*/Progress Reports.
31. "Orientation, U.S.A.—Progress Report," June 1963, *ibid*/Progress Reports.
32. Incident Reports, June 1963, *ibid*/Incidents.
33. "Mr. Kennedy and the Special Protocol Service Section," November 1963, *ibid*/Assassination.
34. For an early but valuable critique of "first step" politics (that also echoed Sanjuan's views), see: Aida DiPace Donald, *John F. Kennedy and the New Frontier* (New York, 1966).
35. "Mr. Kennedy and the Special Protocol Service Section," November 1963, JFK Library, Papers of Pedro Sanjuan, MS78-21/Assassination.

CHAPTER 7

Conclusions

"The glory of a next Augustan age.
Of a power leading from its strength and pride,
Of ambition eager to be tried . . . "

Setting an imperial tone, poet Robert Frost announced at Kennedy's inaugural that American greatness was about to be championed around the globe. Kennedy was his and America's young champion. Everything from eternal peace between Arab and Jew to the calming of harsh rhetoric between English and French Canadians was to be resolved within the Kennedy foreign policy.[1] No decision made in the past was written in stone. No vision was too grand. The veterans of World War II had taken power. Empires had once crumbled before them. Communism would crumble as well. It was destiny.

Writing about the enthusiasm of Special Forces and Peace Corps volunteers in the early 1960s, author Henry Fairlie remembered "they were persuaded that they could stand on the walls of freedom across the world, enjoying the sensation of empire, exalted by the mission which had fallen to them but never to bear the pain."[2] Was the New Frontier a triumph of American arrogance, a smokescreen for Augustan ambitions? John Kenneth Galbraith saw no significance in the answer. He remembered "enormous pride in public service," not imperial designs. "A sense of youth and purpose," he said, was later confused with arrogance.[3] To Pierre Salinger, it was irrelevant to view Kennedy foreign policy from the perspective of youthful enthusiasm or unleashed arrogance. Kennedy's foreign affairs machinery, he concluded, "had already laid the groundwork for a world very different from, and very much better than, the one we live in today."[4] That accomplishment was more important, he stressed, than later perceptions of youthful bumbling and misguided belligerency.

Much of the confusion here was rooted in the conflict of practical versus visionary policies. It was nothing new. Woodrow Wilson's dream of a cooperative world was hampered by his unhappy relationship with Congress and by the commitment to champion a foreign policy rigidly defined by the White House alone. Franklin Roosevelt's vision of the wartime Grand Coalition continuing after World War II was already limited by antitotalitarian policies and suspicious domestic opinion. Even twenty years after Kennedy, Ronald Reagan's dream of an unassailable American military guaranteed by a massive arms buildup lacked practical focus in the era of Soviet soul-searching and collapse. Kennedy's visionary versus practical dilemma appears glaring largely because his determination to win the cold war was based more on patriotic optimism than anything else. Although he would be one of the first to admit it, America's youngest elected president maintained unduly high expectations of himself and the nation. Hence, there was always an irony in his peddling of new, yet cautious "first step" policies. At least, through this method, an eager young politician could rarely lose.

Be it the Peace Corps or even Vietnam, Kennedy handled his foreign policy making with a certain irreverence. Winning the cold war was a heady task, and the electorate appreciated his eloquent commitment to that task, but the multitude of schemes and plans never guaranteed success. Since cold war victory always threatened nuclear destruction, only the daily reality of this ugly threat offered any certitude. In the tradition of New Deal experimentalism, the Kennedy White House would try a variety of foreign policies, deem them brilliant, and target 1970, one year past a projected two-term presidency, as the year of final success.

Success for the Kennedy foreign policy involved crisis management, even though that ever-present nuclear threat loomed high throughout the Berlin and Cuban crises. Kennedy succeeded with his basic objectives in Berlin and Cuba, while the Soviets reassessed their position and view of the allegedly weak, young president. Of course, such matters heightened the cold war, providing, as Kennedy himself noted, only "survivors" and not victors. The resulting Nuclear Test Ban Treaty suggested that a peaceful lesson had been learned from the U.S.-U.S.S.R. confrontation, but Kennedy still sought victory. He hinted to the electorate that even more adventurous policies were around the corner.

Kennedy never turned that corner, and the great adventure would be Vietnam. The historical and political community continues to reel over what Kennedy "might have" done in Vietnam. Researchers will probably find even more interesting quotations by Kennedy to a friend or an associate that outlined the president's thinking on military withdrawal or victory. Still the record remains clear. By November 22, 1963, Kennedy had not yet made an irreversible Vietnam decision. As always, he considered the merit of several options, sharing his thoughts with others. Since he escalated the American military presence in Vietnam and became embroiled in the internal anti-Ho Chi Minh concerns of Saigon politicos and military figures, many conclude that Kennedy would have taken the same tack as his successors. Nevertheless, Kennedy doubted the wisdom of military commitments to Saigon. This will always persuade some to conclude, from the distance of a generation, that, no matter what Kennedy decided, the New Frontier's analytical powers and sense of doing the right thing would have prevailed eventually.

Doing the right thing would have involved educating the cold war–propagandized voter to accept limited goals in American foreign policy. Even if more troops were sent to Vietnam in 1964, the education process could bring them home by the 1966 congressional elections. If that process was successful, the 1966 elections would not be a painful experience for the Democratic party, and the cold war could be proclaimed in a winding down phase. Would this approach have made cold war victory easier to declare as Kennedy's second term came to an end? Again, the possibilities were discussed in cabinet, but the survivors of the Kennedy White House, most of whom went on to serve Lyndon Johnson, apparently forgot the days of discussion and debate.

More than all the tested formulas for cold war victory, the Kennedy foreign policy should be remembered for its effort to build those formulas. Kennedy placed important value on full analysis, intellectual merit, and practical options. Some have denounced this procedure as a waste of time, for it led to near nuclear confrontation. Meanwhile, the policy's chief formulator spent his free time in the arms of various questionable women, according to psycho-historian and moralist, Nigel Hamilton. Thus, Kennedy was both dangerous and immoral.[4] He was, it is said, the direct opposite of the caring, honest intellectual image he projected.

The dangerous/immoral Kennedy is a recent assessment, a product of Vietnam/Watergate cynicism and the latest prurient standard for political behavior. Kennedy's handling of foreign affairs raises questions of experience and efficiency at the height of cold war tensions. The "dangerous" label suggests difficult-to-define plots and scams unleashed on an unsuspecting world by the Harvard elitists of the New Frontier. There is little evidence to suggest these developments, and the world had little difficulty figuring out New Frontier ambitions. The immoral label can be truly applied if solid evidence is found to link Kennedy's sexual appetite to allegedly poor policy making. Even the most comprehensive work on Kennedy as the immoral president, Thomas Reeves's *A Question of Character: John F. Kennedy in Image and Reality* (New York, 1991), admits difficulty in finding the precise relationship between personal character and national leadership. Reeves's book serves as a fine referendum in locating that relationship, and, by no means, is the last word on the subject.

Although his character has become tainted via the changing leadership standards of the 1990s, and his policies savaged by both the political left and right, Kennedy continues to be honored for his intelligence and vision. Considering the level of criticism, that positive memory or legacy remains remarkable. Indeed, much of the New Frontier was attached to clever 1960 campaigning and youthful enthusiasm. But the vision of a "can do" America, for better or worse, wedded to a spirit of commitment and volunteerism, continues to serve as a beacon to foreign policy reformers and activists. Once in power, those reformists and activists can use the practical lessons of the New Frontier, i.e., the limits of American power, the folly of nuclear threats, and the trauma of no-win brushfire war, to move forward with a twenty-first century American foreign policy. Kennedy did little with his own vision for his own generation. Now, he transcends a century.

ENDNOTES

1. Douglas Little, "From Even-Handed to Empty Handed: Seeking Order in the Middle East," and J. L. Granatstein, "When Push Came to Shove: Canada

and the United States," in Paterson, ed., *Kennedy's Quest for Victory*, pp. 156–177, 86–104.
2. Fairlie, *Kennedy Promise*, p. 288
3. "Idealism's Rebirth," *U.S. News and World Report*, Vol. 105, No. 16 (October 24, 1988), pp. 37–40.
4. Nigel Hamilton, *JFK: Reckless Youth* (New York, 1992), pp. xix–xxiv.

BIBLIOGRAPHY

PRIMARY UNPUBLISHED MATERIAL

The Library of President John F. Kennedy, Boston, Massachusetts

Collections:
Senate Files
Biographical Files
President's Official Files (POF)
National Security Files (NSF)
Guam and Pacific Files
White House Central Files
Personal Papers of Cabinet and Staff
Departments and Agencies

National Archives, Washington, D.C.

Collection:
Record Group 273, Records of the National Security Council, 1961–1963

Micronesian Area Research Center (Guam)

Collection:
Confidential Files of the Pacific Collection

State Historical Society of Wisconsin

Collection: Gaylord Nelson Papers

Dissertation

Nurse, Ron. "America Must Not Sleep: The Development of John F. Kennedy's Foreign Policy Attitudes, 1947–1960." Unpublished Ph.D. dissertation, Michigan State University, 1971.

ANALYTICAL, NARRATIVE, AND PUBLISHED PRIMARY WORKS

Books

Ambrose, Stephen. *Eisenhower the President* (New York: Simon & Schuster, 1984).

Arend, Anthony Clark. *Pursuing a Just and Durable Peace: John Foster Dulles and International Organization* (New York: Greenwood, 1988).

Ball, Desmond. *Politics and Force Levels: The Strategic Missile Program of the Kennedy Administration* (Berkeley, CA: University of California Press, 1980).

Ball, George. *The Past Has Another Pattern* (New York: Norton, 1982).

Blair, Joan, and Clay Blair. *The Search for JFK* (New York: Berkley, 1976).

Bowles, Chester. *Promises to Keep* (New York: Harper & Row, 1971).

Brands, H. W., Jr. *Cold Warriors: Eisenhower's Generation and American Foreign Policy* (New York: Columbia University Press, 1988).

Brown, Eugene. *J. William Fulbright: Advice and Dissent* (Iowa City: University of Iowa Press, 1985).

Buchan, John. *Pilgrim's Way* (New York: Carroll and Graf, 1920).

Burke, John P., and Fred I. Greenstein. *How Presidents Test Reality: Decisions on Vietnam, 1954 and 1965* (New York: Russell Sage, 1989).

Burner, David. *John F. Kennedy and a New Generation* (Glenview, IL: Scott, Foresman and Co., 1988).

Burner, David, and Thomas R. West. *The Torch is Passed: The Kennedy Brothers and American Liberalism* (New York: Atheneum, 1984).

Burns, James MacGregor. *John Kennedy: A Political Profile* (New York: Harcourt, Brace, 1960).

Burns, James MacGregor. *The Power to Lead* (New York: Simon and Schuster, 1984).

Casey, Susan Berry. *Hart and Soul* (Concord: NHI Press, 1986).

Catudal, Honoré M. *Kennedy and the Berlin Wall Crisis: A Case Study in U.S. Decision Making* (Berlin: Berlin Verlag, 1980).

Clapp, Priscilla, and Morton Haperin, eds. *United States–Japanese Relations: The 1970s* (Cambridge, MA: Harvard University Press, 1974).

Cohen, Warren I. *Dean Rusk* (Totowa, NJ: Cooper Square, 1980).

Collier, Peter, and David Horowitz. *The Kennedys* (New York: Summit Books, 1984).

Donald, Aida DiPace. *John F. Kennedy and the New Frontier* (New York: Hill and Wang, 1966).

The Editors of *Congressional Quarterly. China–U.S. Policy Since 1945* (Washington, DC: Government Printing Office, 1980).

Eisenhower, Dwight. *The White House Years, Vol. II: Waging Peace, 1956–1961* (Garden City, NY: Doubleday, 1965).

Fairlie, Henry. *The Kennedy Promise: The Politics of Expectation* (New York: Doubleday, 1973).

Finger, Seymour Maxwell. *Your Man at the UN: People, Politics, and Bureaucracy in Making Foreign Policy* (New York: New York University Press, 1980).

Fuchs, Lawrence. *John F. Kennedy and American Catholicism* (New York: Meredith Press, 1967).

Gaddis, John Lewis. *Strategies of Containment* (New York: Oxford University Press, 1982).

George, Alexander, and Richard Swake. *Deterrence in American Foreign Policy, Theory and Practice* (New York: Columbia University Press, 1974).

Goodwin, Doris Kearns. *The Fitzgeralds and the Kennedys* (New York: Simon and Schuster, 1987).

Halperin, Morton H. *Nuclear Fallacy: Dispelling the Myth of Nuclear Strategy* (Cambridge, MA: Harvard University Press, 1987).

Hamilton, Nigel. *JFK: Reckless Youth* (New York: Random House, 1992).

Hammer, Ellen J. *A Death in November: America in Vietnam, 1963* (New York: Oxford University Press, 1987).

Hanson, Simon G. *Dollar Diplomacy Modern Style: Chapters in the Failure of the Alliance for Progress* (Washington, DC: Inter-American Affairs Press, 1970).

Hargreaves, Mary W. M. *The Presidency of John Quincy Adams* (Lawrence: University of Kansas Press, 1985).

Harper, Paul, and Joann P. Krieg, eds. *John F. Kennedy: The Promise Revisited* (Westport: Greenwood Press, 1988).

Hellman, John. *American Myth aid the Legacy of Vietnam* (New York: Columbia University Press, 1986).

Higgins, Trumbull. *The Perfect Failure: Kennedy, Eisenhower, and the CIA at the Bay of Pigs* (New York: Norton, 1987).

Hilsman, Roger. *To Move a Nation: The Politics of Foreign Policy in the Administration of John F. Kennedy* (New York: Doubleday, 1967).

Hodgson, Godfrey. *America in Our Time* (New York: Vintage Books, 1976).

Hoxie, R. Gordon. *Command Decisions and the Presidency: A Study in National Security Policy and Organization* (New York: Center for the Study of the Presidency, 1977).

Humphrey, Hubert H. *Education of a Public Man* (Garden City, NY: Doubleday, 1976).

Jain, R. K. *China and Japan, 1944–76* (Atlantic Highlands, NJ: Humanities Press, 1977).

Janis, Irving. *Groupthink: Phychological Studies of Policy Decisions and Fiascoes* (Boston: Houghton-Mifflin, 1982).

Johnson, Walter, ed. *The Papers of Adlai E. Stevenson*, Vol. 6 (Boston: Little, Brown, 1976).

Jonas, Manfred. *The United States and Germany: A Diplomatic History* (Ithaca: Cornell University Press, 1984).

Jones, Howard. *Indonesia: The Possible Dream* (New York: Harcourt, Brace, Jovanovich, 1971).

Kahn, Herbert. *The Emerging Japanese Superstate* (Englewood Cliffs, NJ: Prentice-Hall, 1970).

Kaplan, Fred. *The Wizards of Armageddon* (New York: Simon & Schuster, 1983).

Kaufman, William. *The McNamara Strategy* (New York: Harper, 1964).

Kelley, Kitty. *Jackie Oh!* (Secaucus, NJ: Ballantine, 1978).

Kennedy, John F. *Profiles in Courage* (New York: Harper, 1956).

Kennedy, John F. *Public Papers of the President, 1961–1963* (Washington, DC: Government Printing Office, 1962–1964).

Kennedy, John F. *Why England Slept* (New York: Widred Funk, 1940).

Kennedy, Robert F. *Thirteen Days* (New York: Norton, 1969).

Kern, Montague, Patricia W. Levering, and Ralph B. Levering. *The Kennedy Crises: The Press, the Presidency, and Foreign Policy* (Chapel Hill: University of North Carolina Press, 1983).

Kolko, Gabriel. *Anatomy of a War: Vietnam, The United States, and the Modern Historical Experience* (New York: Pantheon, 1985).

Koskoff, David. *Joseph P. Kennedy* (Englewood Cliffs, NJ: Prentice-Hall, 1974).

Lederer, William J., and Eugene Burdick. *The Ugly American* (New York: Norton, 1960).

Lee, Dwight E., ed. *Munich: Blunder, Plot, or Tragic Necessity?* (Lexington, MA: D.C. Heath, 1970).

Lowi, Theodore J. *The Personal President: Power Invested, Promise Unfulfilled* (Ithaca: Cornell University Press, 1985).

Maga, Timothy P. *John F. Kennedy and the New Pacific Community, 1961–1963* (New York: Macmillan/St. Martin's Press, 1990).

Mahoney, Richard. *JFK: Ordeal in Africa* (New York: Oxford University Press, 1983).

Manchester, William. *Remembering Kennedy: One Brief and Shining Moment* (Boston: Little, Brown, 1983).

Matusow, Allen J. *The Unraveling of America: A History of Liberalism in the 1960s* (New York: Harper, 1984).

Medland, William J. *The Cuban Missile Crisis of 1962: Needless or Necessary?* (New York: Greenwood, 1988).

Melanson, Richard A., and David Mayers, eds. *Reevaluating Eisenhower: American Foreign Policy in the 1950s* (Urbana: University of Illinois Press, 1987).

Merli, Frank, and Theodore A. Wilson, eds. *Makers of American Diplomacy*, Vols. 1 & 2 (New York: Scribners, 1974).

Neustadt, Richard E. *Presidential Power and the Modern Presidents: The Politics of Leadership from Roosevelt to Reagan* (New York: Free Press, 1990).

Noer, Thomas. *Cold War and Black Liberation: The United States and*

White Rule in Africa, 1948–1968 (Columbia, MO: University of Missouri Press, 1985).

Nolting, Frederick. *From Trust to Tragedy: The Political Memoirs of Frederick Nolting, Kennedy's Ambassador to Diem's Vietnam* (Westport, CT: Greenwood, 1988).

O'Brien, Lawrence. *No Final Victories* (New York: Doubleday, 1974).

O'Donnell, Kenneth, and David F. Powers. *"Johnny, We Hardly Knew Ye"* (Boston: Little, Brown, 1970).

Palmer, Bruce. *The 25 Year War: America's Military Role in Vietnam* (Lexington: University Press of Kentucky, 1984).

Parkenham, Robert A. *Liberal American and the Third World* (Princeton, NJ: Princeton University Press, 1973).

Parmet, Herbert. *Jack: The Struggles of John F. Kennedy* (New York: Dial Press, 1980).

Parmet, Herbert S. *JFK: The Presidency of John F. Kennedy* (New York: Dial Press, 1983).

Passin, Herbert, ed. *The United States and Japan* (Englewood Cliffs, NJ: Prentice-Hall, 1966).

Pastor, Robert. *Congress and the Politics of U.S. Foreign Economic Policy, 1929–1976* (Berkeley: University of California Press, 1980).

Paterson, Thomas G., ed. *Kennedy's Quest for Victory: American Foreign Policy, 1961–1963* (New York: Oxford University Press, 1989).

Patti, Achimedes L. A. *Why Vietnam? Prelude to America's Albatross* (Berkley: University of California Press, 1980).

Rabe, Stephen G. *Eisenhower and Latin America: The Foreign Policy of Anti-Communism* (Chapel Hill: University of North Carolina Press, 1988).

Ranney, Austin. *Channels of Power: The Impact of Television on American Politics* (New York: Basic Books, 1983).

Rapoport, Ronald B., Alan I. Abramowitz, and John McClennon, eds. *The Life of the Parties: Activists in Presidential Politics* (Lexington: University Press of Kentucky, 1986).

Reeves, Thomas C. *A Question of Character: John F. Kennedy in Image and Reality* (New York: Free Press, 1991).

Reischauer, Edwin. *Beyond Vietnam: The United States and Asia* (New York: Knopf, 1967).

Rice, Gerald T. *The Bold Experiment* (South Bend, IN: University of Notre Dame Press, 1985).

Rice, Gerald T. *Twenty Years of Peace Corps* (Washington, DC: Government Printing Office, 1981).

Roberts, Priscilla, ed. *Sino–American Relations Since 1900* (Hong Kong: University of Hong Kong Press, 1991).

Rostow, Walt. *The Diffusion of Power* (New York: Macmillan, 1972).

Rostow, Walt. *Stages of Economic Growth: A Non-Communist Manifesto* (New York: Cambridge University Press, 1974).

Rust, William. *Kennedy in Vietnam* (New York: Charles Scribner's Sons, 1985).

Salinger, Pierre. *With Kennedy* (Garden City, NY: Doubleday, 1966).

Schlesinger, Arthur M., Jr. *A Thousand Days: John F. Kennedy in the White House* (Boston: Houghton Mifflin, 1965).

Schlesinger, Arthur M., Jr. *The Cycles of American History* (Boston: Houghton Mifflin, 1986).

Schlesinger, Arthur M., Jr. *Kennedy or Nixon?: Does it Make Any Difference?* (New York: Macmillan, 1960).

Schlesinger, Arthur M., Jr. *Robert Kennedy and His Times* (Boston: Houghton Mifflin, 1978).

Schoenbaum, Thomas. *Waging Peace and War: Dean Rusk in the Truman, Kennedy, and Johnson Years* (New York: Simon & Schuster, 1988).

Seaborg, Glenn T. *Kennedy, Khrushchev and the Test Ban* (Berkeley: University of California Press, 1981).

Shriver, Sargent. *Point of the Lance* (New York: Harper & Row, 1964.

Slusser, Robert. *The Berlin Crisis of 1961* (Baltimore: Johns Hopkins University Press, 1971).

Smith, Craig Allen, and Kathy B. Smith, eds. *The President and the Public: Rhetoric and National Leadership*, Vol. 7: *The Credibility of Institutions, Policies, and Leadership* (Lanham, MD: University Press of America, 1985).

Smith, Ralph B. *An International History of the Vietnam War*, Vol. 1: *Revolution versus Containment, 1955–61* and Vol. 2: *The Kennedy Strategy* (New York: St. Martin's Press, 1983).

Snyder, J. Richard, ed. *John F. Kennedy: Person, Policy, Presidency* (Wilmington, DE: Scholarly Resources, 1988).

Sorenson, Theodore C. *Kennedy* (New York: Harper, 1965).

Sorenson, Theodore C. *The Kennedy Legacy* (New York: Macmillan, 1969).

Thompson, Kenneth W., ed. *The Kennedy Presidency* (Lanham, MD: University Press of America, 1985).

Trewhitt, Henry. *McNamara* (New York: Harper, 1971).

U.S. Congress. *Congressional Quarterly Almanac, 1963* (Washington, DC: Government Printing Office, 1964).

U.S. Congress. *Executive Sessions of the Senate Foreign Relations Committee Together With Joint Sessions with the Senate Armed Services Committee, 1961–64*, Vols. XIII–XVI (Washington, DC: Government Printing Office, 1985–88).

U.S. Congress. *John F. Kennedy: A Compilation of Statements and Speeches Made during His Service in the United States Senate and House of Representatives* (Washington, DC: Government Printing Office, 1964).

U.S. Congress, Senate. *The American Overseas. Hearings Before the Committee on Foreign Relations*, 86th Congress, 1st Session (Washington, DC: Government Printing Office, 1959–60).

U.S. House of Representatives Committee on Armed Services. *United States–Vietnam Relations, 1945–67* (Washington, DC: Government Printing Office, 1971).

Wagner, R. Harrison. *United States Policy Toward Latin America* (Stanford: Stanford University Press, 1970).

Walton, Richard. *Cold War and Counterrevolution: The Foreign Policy of John F. Kennedy* (New York: Viking, 1972).

Ward, John W. *Red, White and Blue: Men, Books, and Ideas in American Culture* (New York: Oxford University Press, 1969).

Watanabe, Akio. *The Okinawa Problem: A Chapter in Japan–U.S. Relations* (Carlton, Australia: Melbourne University Press, 1970).

Wayne, Stephen. *The Road to the White House: The Politics of Presidential Elections* (New York: St. Martin's Press, 1984).

Welch, Richard. *Response to Revolution: The United States and the Cuban Revolution, 1959–61* (Chapel Hill: University of North Carolina Press, 1985).

Whalen, Richard. *The Founding Father* (New York: New American Library, 1964).

White, Theodore H. *The Making of the President, 1960* (New York: Atheneum, 1967).

Williams, G. Mennen. *Africa for the Africans* (Grand Rapids, MI: Eerdmans, 1969).

Wills, Garry. *The Kennedy Imprisonment: A Meditation on Power* (Boston: Little, Brown, 1982).

Wilson, Joan Hoff, and Marjorie Lightman. *Without Precedent: The*

Life and Career of Eleanor Roosevelt (Bloomington: Indiana University Press, 1984).

Wofford, Harris. *Of Kennedys and Kings* (New York: Farrar, Straus, and Giroux, 1980).

Wyden, Peter. *Bay of Pigs: The Untold Story* (New York: Simon and Schuster, 1979).

Yanaga, Chitoshi. *Big Business in Japanese Politics* (New Haven: Yale University Press, 1968).

Articles

"A Dreamer Wide Awake," *American Heritage*, Vol. 16, October 1965, p. 81.

Anderson, Paul. "Decision-Making by Objection and the Cuban Missile Crisis," *Administration Quarterly*, Vol. 28, June 1983, pp. 201–222.

Buttinger, Joseph. "Fact and Fiction on Foreign Aid: A Critique of 'The Ugly American' " *Dissent, A Quarterly of Socialist Opinion*, Vol. 6, Summer 1959, pp. 319–320.

Chang, Gordon. "JFK, China, and the Bomb," *Journal of American History*, Vol. 74, March 1988, pp. 1287–1310.

Cronin, Thomas. "On the American Presidency: A Conversation with James MacGregor Burns," *Presidential Studies Quarterly*, Vol. XVI, No. 3, Summer 1986, pp. 528–542.

Gordon, Leonard H. D. "United States Opposition to the Use of Force in the Taiwan Strait, 1954–1962," *The Journal of American History*, Vol. 72, No. 3, December 1985, pp. 637–660.

Hafner, Donald C. "Bureaucratic Politics and 'Those Frigging Missiles,' " *Orbis*, Vol. 21, Summer 1977, p. 307–333.

"JFK: His Vision, Then and Now;" "Beyond the Generations;" "A Time for Self-Interest;" and Thomas Moore & Marianna Knight "Idealism's Rebirth;" *U.S. News and World Report*, Vol. 105, No. 16, October 24, 1988, pp. 32–40.

Kennan, George. "Japan's Security and American Policy," *Foreign Affairs*, Vol. 43, October 1964, 14–28.

Kennedy, John F. "If the Soviets Control Space—They Control Earth," *Missiles and Rockets*, Vol. 7, October 10, 1960, pp. 12–13.

Maga, Timothy P. "Humanism and Peace: Eleanor Roosevelt's Mission to the Pacific, August–September, 1943" *The Maryland Historian*, Vol. XIX, No. 2, Fall/Winter 1988, pp. 33–47.

Maga, Timothy P. "The New Frontier vs. Guided Democracy: JFK, Sukarno, and Indonesia, 1961–1963," *Presidential Studies Quarterly*, Vol. XX, Winter 1990, pp. 91–102.

"McNamara Faults Cuba for Tensions with U.S.," *Boston Globe*, January 10, 1992, p. 2.

Nathan, James. "The Missile Crisis: His Finest Hour Now," *World Politics*, Vol. 27, January 1975, p. 263.

"Nomination Text," *The Washington Post*, September 13, 1960, p. A16.

Nurse, Ronald. "Critic of Colonialism: JFK and Algerian Independence," *The Historian*, Vol. 39, February 1977, pp. 307–326.

Paterson, Thomas. "October Missiles and November Elections: The Cuban Missile Crisis and American Poitics, 1962," *Journal of American History*, Vol. 73, No. 1, June 1986, pp. 87–119.

Pelz, Stephen. "John F. Kennedy's 1961 Vietnam War Decisions," *Journal of Strategic Studies*, Vol. 4, December 1981, pp. 356–385.

Rawson, D. W. "Foreign Policy and Australian Parties," *World Review*, July 1962, pp. 16–23.

Reischauer, Edwin O. "The Broken Dialogue with Japan," *Foreign Affairs*, Vol. 39, October 1960, pp. 11–16.

Thomson, James C., Jr. "On the Making of U.S. China Policy, 1961–1969: A Study in Bureaucratic Politics," *China Quarterly*, Vol. 50, April–June 1972, pp. 221–222.

"The Ugly American," *The Nation*, October 4, 1958, p. 199.

"The Ugly American," *The Saturday Evening Post*, November 8, 1958, p. 4.

Wilcynski, J. "Australia's Trade with China," *India Quarterly*, April–June 1965, pp. 154–167.

Wofford, Harris. "The Future of the Peace Corps," *Annals of the American Academy of Political and Social Science*, JFK Library Courtesy Copy, 1970.

Zeiler, Thomas. "Free Trade Politics and Diplomacy," *Diplomatic History*, Vol. XI, Spring 1987, pp. 127–142.

INDEX